STIRLING'S DESERT TRIUMPH

The SAS Egyptian Airfield Raids 1942

GAVIN MORTIMER

First published in Great Britain in 2015 by Osprey Publishing,
PO Box 883, Oxford, OX1 9PL, UK
1385 Broadway, 5th Floor, New York, NY 10018, USA
E-mail: info@ospreypublishing.com

Osprey Publishing is part of Bloomsbury Publishing Plc

A CIP catalogue record for this book is available from the British Library

Print ISBN: 978 1 4728 0763 2
PDF ebook ISBN: 978 1 4728 0764 9
ePub ebook ISBN: 978 1 4728 0765 6

Index by Sharon Redmayne
Typeset in Sabon
Map by bounford.com
3D BEV by Alan Gilliland
Originated by PDQ Media, Bungay, UK
Printed in China through Worldprint Ltd

16 17 18 19   10 9 8 7 6 5 4 3

Osprey Publishing is supporting the Woodland Trust, the UK's leading
woodland conservation charity, by funding the dedication of trees.

www.ospreypublishing.com

PHOTOS

All photos in this book are courtesy of the SAS Regimental Association

CONTENTS

INTRODUCTION

On 21 June 1942 Gen Erwin Rommel issued an Order of the Day to the men under his command:

Soldiers!

The great battle in the Marmarica has been crowned by your quick conquest of Tobruk. We have taken in all over 45,000 prisoners and destroyed or captured more than 1,000 armoured fighting vehicles and nearly 400 guns. During your long hard struggle of the last four weeks, you have, through your incomparable courage and tenacity, dealt the enemy blow upon blow. Your spirit of attack has cost him the core of his field army, which was standing poised for an offensive. Above all, he has lost his powerful armour. My special congratulations to officers and men for this superb achievement.

Soldiers of the Panzer Army Afrika!

Now for the complete destruction of the enemy. We will not rest until we have shattered the last remnants of the British Eighth Army. During the days to come, I shall call on you for one more great effort to bring us to this final goal.

ROMMEL

The Prime Minister, Winston Churchill, was in Washington when he learned of the fall of Tobruk. His trip to the United States had been intended as an opportunity to build on his relationship with President Franklin D. Roosevelt; instead Churchill had to confront Britain's gravest crisis since the black days of the Battle of Britain two years earlier. 'Into the Middle East for three years the British Empire had poured every man, gun and tank it could spare,' wrote the noted Australian war correspondent Alan Moorehead, who had first arrived in Cairo in June 1940. 'Here alone the British had a front against the enemy. The loss of Egypt would precipitate a chain of misfortunes almost too disastrous to contemplate.'

But contemplate them Moorehead did, as Churchill did too. If Rommel's Afrika Korps conquered Egypt, then Britain would lose Malta and with it control of the Mediterranean. The Suez Canal would also fall into German

11 JANUARY 1941

Hitler's Directive 22 creates the Afrika Korps

hands, imperilling Palestine and Syria and, in the longer term, India and the Soviet Union.

As the British quailed, Rommel pushed east, reaching Sidi Barrani by the evening of 24 June and the next day advancing to within forty miles of Mersa Matruh. On the last day of the month Rommel approached the El Alamein line, just 65 miles west of Egypt's second city of Alexandria. The British fleet had already fled the coastal city and all officers received orders to rejoin their units immediately. Meanwhile in Cairo, recalled Moorehead, 'the streets were jammed with cars that had evacuated from Alexandria and … the British consulate was besieged with people seeking visas to Palestine. The eastbound Palestine trains were jammed. A thin mist of smoke hung over the British embassy by the Nile and over the sprawling blocks of GHQ – huge quantities of secret documents were being burnt.'

The Phantom Major

In Cairo at this time was a young Scottish major named David Stirling. While Rommel had been overrunning Tobruk, Stirling and a handful of men

The Germans nicknamed Stirling 'The Phantom Major', such was his ability to ghost on to airfields, wreak havoc and then vanish without a trace.

The Afrika Korps' arrival in the Western Desert in early 1941 made life more difficult for the British after their easy defeat of the Italian Army in 1940.

from L Detachment, Special Air Service Brigade, were busy attacking aircraft and shipping in the Benghazi–Berca–Benina area, the latter being the Germans' chief repair base for their aircraft, approximately 700 miles west of Alexandria.

From Benina, the SAS raiders were transported in 30cwt Chevrolet trucks, driven by the Long Range Desert Group (LRDG), south-east to their desert base at Siwa Oasis, arriving on 21 June to learn of the fall of Tobruk. Instructing his men to withdraw to Kabrit, the SAS training base 90 miles east of Cairo on the edge of the Great Bitter Lake, Stirling headed to the Egyptian capital to see how he could be of help.

Amid the gloom and despondency at GHQ, Stirling was able to inform his superior that in the last six months the SAS had destroyed at least 143 Axis aircraft as well as laying waste to numerous petrol bowsers, repair bases and bomb dumps. It was even rumoured that the Germans had a name for Stirling, 'The Phantom Major', such was his ability to ghost on to airfields, wreak havoc and then vanish without a trace.

Stirling's arrival in Cairo coincided with the decision of Gen Claude Auchinleck, Commander-in-Chief Middle East, to sack Neil Ritchie as commander of the Eighth Army and take on the role himself. Auchinleck was planning a counter-attack against Rommel to regain the coastal region around Mersa Matruh, and with this in mind he instructed Stirling, supported by patrols of the LRDG, to concentrate his unit at Qaret Tartura on the north-western edge of the Qattara Depression. From this remote base Stirling was ordered to attack airfields and enemy lines of communication

in the Fuka–Bagush area, about 55 miles west of El Alamein, as the Eighth Army went on the counter-attack to drive Rommel west.

Stirling's second-in-command, Capt Blair 'Paddy' Mayne, a huge man who had played international rugby for Ireland before the war, suggested to his commander that 'it would be useful if a jeep could be provided to transport the elements of the Special Air Service Regiment to the scene of the operations'. Stirling liked the idea and managed to procure 15 American-built Willys Bantam jeeps.

Another SAS officer, Capt Lord Jellicoe, recalled that throughout this trying time Auchinleck was 'sanguine' despite the close proximity of the enemy, although 'Stirling, as force commander, did not share this optimism'.

There was good reason for this, according to Jellicoe, as the SAS had never before been motorised. 'Four days only were available for preparations', he wrote in his operational report of the period. '15 jeeps had to be prepared with special equipment and guns and twenty 3 ton lorries loaded. This meant that the drivers and maintenance crews had to work, for some times, as long as 72 hours almost without a break.'

Consequently, there was a 'great strain imposed on personnel of SAS Regiment and LRDG' in the first week of July as they hurried to get ready for their new phase of guerrilla warfare. Ranged against them was Rommel's Afrika Korps, its soldiers tired but bristling with the same self-confidence as their charismatic commander.

ORIGINS

The Commandos in the Middle East

On 1 February 1941 a large force of British Commandos had sailed for the Middle East aboard three troopships. The commandos had been formed the previous summer, at the behest of Winston Churchill, and the three units en route to Egypt were 7, 8 and 11 Commando. Hitherto 8 Commando had been known as the Guards Commando and among its ranks was Lt David Stirling, a tall, languid young officer known as the 'Giant Sloth' to his peers. Sailing towards the Middle East, Stirling idled away much of his time playing cards with two fellow officers – Randolph Churchill, son of the Prime Minister, and the writer Evelyn Waugh.

The commandos arrived at Geneifa, on the edge of the Suez Canal, on 11 March, where they were informed by Gen Archibald Wavell, Commander-in-Chief, Middle East Forces, that two further troops of commandos (50 and 52) had been raised in the Middle East and would be added to 7, 8 and 11 Commando to form 'Layforce' under the command of Col Robert Laycock.

When the commandos had sailed from Scotland six weeks earlier the British Army was master of all it surveyed in North Africa. One British officer, Brigadier Desmond Young, wrote that in Egypt 'fat pashas invited senior British officers to the Mahomed Ali Club. There were garden-parties in the gardens of the rich around Gezireh. Cairo society ceased to practise its Italian.'

It was the crushing defeat of Italy in North Africa in only eight months that gave the British (and their Allies) their swagger, the army of Marshal Rodolfo Graziani routed by that of Wavell's. As Young noted, the Western Desert Force, later expanded to form the Eighth Army, had advanced 500 miles in two months and 'beaten and destroyed an Italian army of four corps, comprising nine divisions and part of a tenth. It had captured 13,000 prisoners, 400 tanks and 1,290 guns, beside vast quantities of other material'.

DAVID STIRLING – THE FAILED ARTIST

Born in 1915 in central Scotland, Stirling was one of six children of Gen Archibald Stirling, a veteran of the First World War, and the Honourable Margaret Fraser, fourth daughter of the 13th Baron Lovat. The Stirlings are an ancient, aristocratic family and David enjoyed a privileged upbringing even if it did entail boarding at the austere Ampleforth College. It was there, deep in the North Yorkshire countryside, that Stirling indulged his love of the outdoors as in his vivid imagination 'he tracked wild beasts through the fields and hedgerows'. When he went up to Cambridge in the mid-1930s, Stirling was a gangly young man of 6ft 6in intent on enjoying life to its utmost. He lasted a year at Cambridge before deciding university wasn't for him, so he settled in Paris with the aim of becoming a painter. But Stirling lacked artistic talent, and when told by his tutor to look for another outlet for his creative energies, '[I] was quite shattered as I had honestly believed it was only a matter of time before I smashed the barrier'. Depressed by his failure, Stirling set his sights on scaling Mount Everest, announcing his intention to climb the Himalayan peak. He trained first in the Swiss Alps and then in the Rocky Mountains in the United States. Moving south through Colorado, tackling the ranges in Park Gore and Sawatch, 23-year-old David Stirling interrupted his horse ride south to pay a visit to Las Vegas to win some money at the gaming tables. That done, he continued on towards the Rio Grande, arriving in early September 1939, where he heard the news that Britain and Germany were once more at war.

Stirling, a member of the Scots Guards Supplementary Reserve, returned to Britain and presented himself at the regimental depot in Pirbright. Stirling and the Guards were not a natural fit. The Bohemian side to his character did not sit well with the drill sergeants at Pirbright and on one occasion Stirling was reprimanded for his unclean rifle. 'Stirling, it's bloody filthy. There must be a bloody clown on the end of this rifle,' exclaimed the sergeant. 'Yes, sergeant,' agreed Stirling, 'but not at my end.'

Neither did Stirling endear himself to those senior officers whose job it was to lecture their young protégés on the art of war. Most of them, in Stirling's view, held opinions that had altered little since the First World War, so the young officer spent increasing amounts of his time – and his money – drinking and gambling in London's clubs. When he eventually left Pirbright he was described by his instructors as an 'irresponsible and unremarkable soldier'.

Despite his lack of aptitude for regular soldiering, Stirling wasn't short of belligerence and more than anything he wanted to fight the enemy. In January 1940 the 5th Battalion, the Scots Guards, were sent on a mountain warfare course in the French Alps and rumours abounded that they were going to be sent to help Finland fight the Russians. That mission never materialised and Stirling grew ever more frustrated with what had by now been dubbed 'The Phoney War'. Then one day in the early summer of 1940 Stirling learned that volunteers were wanted for a special service force. He was accepted for the new force and posted to 8 Commando under the command of Robert Laycock. For the first time in his military career Stirling found himself among like-minded soldiers all desperate to have a crack at the Germans.

David Stirling faces the camera. The founder of the SAS rarely sported a moustache.

Enter the Afrika Korps

When news reached Adolf Hitler in Berlin of Italy's capitulation in the Libyan Desert, the Nazi leader was initially indifferent. North Africa was a sideshow, inconsequential in comparison to his ambitions in eastern Europe. It was Admiral Erich Raeder, head of the German Navy, who did most to turn Hitler's attention towards events in North Africa. What, Raeder asked of his Führer, would happen to Germany if the British had an unshakeable grip on the Mediterranean? It would seriously jeopardise Hitler's plans for conquest in the Balkans and the Soviet Union. So it was with reluctance that on 11 January 1941, Hitler issued Directive 22, which Ronald Lewin, British military historian and veteran of the North African campaign, described as 'the birth certificate of the Afrika Korps'.

Directive 22 authorised the raising of a force to be sent to North Africa to support Germany's Italian allies. Codenamed Operation *Sunflower*, the force was designated 5 Light Division. However, it wasn't until 6 February that Hitler gave Gen Erwin Rommel command of the unit. A fortnight later the force was formally reconstituted as the *Deutsches Afrika Korps*, by which time its vanguard had already reached Tripoli in Libya.

Within two months of the arrival of the advance elements, the Afrika Korps achieved spectacular successes in the desert war, what Lewin called 'a true *blitz*, during which it would overrun Cyrenaica [eastern Libya], capture three generals, and so savage an armoured division [2nd] that it would be instantly deleted from the British Order of Battle.' Msus, Mechili, Derna, Sollum, Tmimi and, most significantly of all, the port of Benghazi all fell to the Afrika Korps as the British retreated 30 miles inside the frontier

The Afrika Korps was comprised of excellent soldiers, but it lacked the initiative and imagination to form a comparable special forces unit to rival the SAS.

of Egypt. The only prize that eluded Rommel was the coastal city of Tobruk, which held firm despite repeated German attacks.

The consequences of Rommel's gains had grave repercussions for Layforce. The commandos had been despatched to the Middle East as a flank attack force, to launch raids on enemy targets in Italy, the Balkans and any remaining Italian resistance in North Africa. However, by the time they had finished their training in Egypt they were tasked with attacking important strategic ports now in enemy possession. A Battalion of Layforce, originally 7 Commando, raided the seaport of Bardia on 19 April 'to harass the enemy's L. of C. [lines of communication] and inflict as much damage as possible on supplies and material' (Operation Order, April 19 1941). What unfolded was a fiasco. Some detachments were landed on the wrong beach, while others came ashore behind schedule and aborted their mission.

B Battalion (8 Commando) fared little better in the Middle East. The force was split up and sent either to help in the evacuation of Crete or to reinforce the besieged garrison at Tobruk. The 33 officers and 513 men of C Battalion (11 Scottish Commando), meanwhile, were sent to the Mediterranean island of Cyprus at the end of April in anticipation of a German invasion. A month later they had seen no sight of the enemy and the men were growing disillusioned.

In May 1941 Col Laycock wrote to Arthur Smith, Chief of the General Staff, warning him that 'Our situation is now becoming desperate. When we formed in England we got together a fine body of men who volunteered for daring action which has been continually promised us since last August … [but] unless we are actively employed soon I anticipate a serious falling off in morale which was at one time second to none.'

Despite 11 (Scottish) Commando being sent to Syria in June 1941, where it participated in the offensive against Vichy France forces menacing British interests in the Middle East, that same month it was decided by MEHQ to disband Layforce; its men would either return to their original units or be used as replacements for undermanned regiments in North Africa in readiness for an imminent offensive against Rommel's Afrika Korps.

On learning of Layforce's demise, Stirling wrote to his family in Scotland, informing them: 'The Commandos are no more. I am not sure what I shall do now but I am attempting and may succeed in establishing a permanent parachute unit. It would be on a small scale but would be more amusing than any other form of soldiering.'

INITIAL STRATEGY

L Detachment

Stirling's parachute scheme wasn't just a flight of fancy. Together with Jock Lewes, also of 8 Commando, the pair intercepted a consignment of parachutes destined for India with the idea of forming an airborne unit similar to the German Fallschirmjäger that had fought with such gallantry during the invasion of Crete. Another Layforce veteran, Guardsman Mick D'Arcy, accompanied Lewes and Stirling to collect the parachutes from an RAF officer at a base near Fuka. A few days later the three men jumped from an old Vickers Valencia and D'Arcy threw himself out of the aircraft before Stirling. He was therefore 'surprised to see Lt Stirling pass me in the air'.

Stirling's parachute had caught on the aircraft's tail section as he jumped and he descended at high velocity, hitting the ground with a sickening thud that left him temporarily blinded and paralysed. Despite his lucky escape, Stirling was more convinced than ever of the potential for a parachute unit in the Middle East, and as he recovered from his injuries in Cairo's Scottish General Hospital, he drafted a memo entitled *Case for the retention of a limited number of special service troops, for employment as parachutists.* In a subsequent summary of the memo, Stirling wrote:

The SAS learned to parachute in North Africa in 1941 using Whitley bombers, which involved jumping through a hole in the bottom of the fuselage.

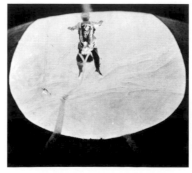

I sought to prove that, if an aerodrome or transport park was the objective of an operation, then the destruction of 50 aircraft or units of transport was more easily accomplished by a sub-unit of five men than by a force of 200 men. I further concluded that 200 properly selected, trained and equipped men, organised into sub-units of five, should be able to attack at least thirty different objectives at the same time on the same night as compared to only one objective using the current Commando technique. So, only 25% success in the former is equivalent to many times the maximum result in the latter.

16 NOVEMBER 1941

'L Detachment, Special Air Service Brigade' carries out its first raid

Upon his release from hospital, Stirling submitted his proposal to Maj Gen Neil Ritchie, Deputy Chief of the General Staff (DCGS), Middle East Forces, who liked what he read. Three days later Stirling was expanding on his idea in person to Gen Claude Auchinleck, the outcome of which was authorisation to recruit six officers and 60 other ranks to a unit named L Detachment of the Special Air Service Brigade, the reason being that if – or more likely when – German intelligence got wind of the incipient force they would believe that a British airborne brigade had deployed to Egypt.

The inaugural SAS raid was an unmitigated disaster. Launched on the night of 16 November 1941, to coincide with the start of Auchinleck's latest offensive against Rommel to seize back control of the eastern coastal regions of Libya, the objective was to parachute behind enemy lines and carry out five simultaneous attacks against Axis forward fighter and bomber airfields between Tmimi and Gazala. The SAS raiders would then rendezvous in the desert with the LRDG, which would transport them to safety.

Unfortunately for Stirling, the raid coincided not just with the start of Operation *Crusader* but also with one of the worst storms to hit the region in years. Of the 55 SAS soldiers who took part in the raid, 34 were either killed or captured, leaving Stirling with just 20 men with which to continue. The SAS was in danger of being stillborn, but Stirling was nothing if not tenacious, and he was also broad-minded enough to listen to the advice of others.

Operations with the LRDG

Among the LRDG patrols that collected the exhausted remnants of the parachute raid was one commanded by Capt David Lloyd-Owen. Over a mug of hot tea Lloyd-Owen suggested to Stirling an alternative to parachuting: the back of an LRDG truck. In future wouldn't it be less hazardous if the LRDG ferried Stirling and his men to the target area? After all, the LRDG had been operating in the region since August 1940 and knew the region better than anyone – British, German or Italian.

Lt Col Guy Prendergast, commanding officer of the LRDG, sanctioned the plan when Stirling and Lloyd-Owen arrived back at Siwa Oasis on 25 November, and suddenly new life was breathed into the SAS.

Meanwhile Gen Auchinleck, seeing that Rommel's supply lines along the Libyan coast were over-extended, ordered two flying columns under the command of Brigadiers Denys Reid and John Marriott to attack the Axis forces hundreds of miles behind the front line as the Eighth Army launched a secondary offensive. To complement these flying columns, Auchinleck instructed the LRDG to attack Axis aerodromes at Sirte, Agheila and

Original members of the SAS wearing hard hats during their parachute training in 1941.

Agedabia. Prendergast saw an opportunity for the SAS to avenge the failure of their first raid and on 28 November sent a signal from his base at Siwa Oasis to MEHQ: 'As LRDG not trained for demolitions, suggest pct [parachutists] used for blowing dromes.' Prendergast's suggestion was accepted and Stirling received permission to launch an overland assault on the aerodromes the following month.

The results were spectacular. A party of seven men, led by Paddy Mayne, destroyed 24 aircraft and a barracks full of Axis pilots at Tamet aerodrome, while Lt Bill Fraser and four men blew up 37 aircraft at Agedabia and returned safely in the care of the LRDG. The irrepressible Mayne paid a second visit to Tamet at the end of December and accounted for 27 planes that had only recently arrived to replace the ones destroyed on his previous visit to the airfield.

But despite Mayne's success there was an incident that emphasised the raiders' vulnerability in attacking airfields on foot. One of the fuses on their bombs exploded prematurely – after 22 minutes instead of 30 – and the SAS party were illuminated by the flames as they slipped from the scene. They withdrew successfully but Jock Lewes wasn't so fortunate. His small force had been attacked by a marauding Messerschmitt on their return from a raid on Nofilia aerodrome and Lewes was killed by the aircraft's cannon fire.

Lewes was Stirling's unofficial second-in-command, and his death robbed the SAS of its most ingenious member (Lewes had invented the eponymous bomb of plastic explosive and thermite that was used in their raids). Nonetheless, the unit continued to expand with Auchinleck agreeing in early 1942 to Stirling's request to recruit six more officers and up to 40 men.

In addition Stirling acquired the rank of Major (Mayne was promoted Captain and both received the DSO) as well as a detachment of 50 French paratroopers recently arrived in the Middle East from Britain. One of the Frenchmen was Roger Boutinot, before the war an assistant in a St Malo patisserie before sailing to England to escape the invading Germans. 'We did a lot of marching across the desert and a lot of explosives training and sabotage work,' he remembered of his early days at Kabrit with the SAS. 'Every morning sergeant major [Gus] Glaze took us for PT. Everybody went, British and French. We played basketball against the English, and football. The camaraderie was excellent.'

Morale was also good, and L Detachment acquired its own sand-coloured beret and insignia around this time. Sgt Bob Tait was responsible for the cap badge insignia, the flaming sword of Excalibur (the 'winged dagger' misnomer was started by a 2SAS officer Roy Farran, a flamboyant character who published his war memoirs in 1948 as *Winged Dagger* for no other reason than it sounded more martial), while Stirling came up with the 'Who Dares Wins' motto.

By early January 1942 Rommel had been driven out of Cyrenaica and had retreated as far west as Tripolitania. However, this time it was the British who had overreached themselves – a situation caused in part by events in the

Jumping off the back of trucks was one of the ways by which the SAS learned the rudiments of parachuting. This photograph was taken in the summer of 1941.

PADDY MAYNE – THE FIGHTER OF FEW WORDS

Blair Mayne, or 'Paddy' to the men who served with him in the Special Air Service, was a ferocious soldier and a phenomenal athlete. A university heavyweight boxing champion, the Ulster-born Mayne was an even better rugby union player, winning his first cap for Ireland in 1938. On the strength of his performances that season for Ireland, the 23-year-old lock forward was chosen to tour South Africa in the summer with the British and Irish Lions. Mayne, who stood 6ft 3in and weighed 16st, played in 19 of the tour's 24 matches, including all three Test matches against South Africa, and was the pick of the tourists. Dougie Morkel, one of the legendary figures of early South African rugby, described Mayne as 'the finest all-round forward I have ever seen and he is magnificently built for the part. In staying power he has to be seen to be believed'.

But there was another side to Mayne that appeared during the tour to South Africa, one that would emerge also during his time with the SAS. The Irishman liked a drink and more often than not his boozing would end in a brawl. One of Mayne's Lions' teammates, Vivian Jenkins, recalled that: 'He was a very quiet chap ... at first glance you would think he wouldn't hurt a fly but we soon discovered that when he got steamed up, he would do anything.'

Had it not been for the outbreak of war, Mayne might well have had a nondescript working life as a Belfast solicitor, but in April 1940 he enlisted in the Royal Ulster Rifles and two months later became one of the first volunteers for the incipient commandos. Posted to 11 (Scottish) Commando (later subsumed into Layforce), Mayne distinguished himself at the battle of Litani River in Syria in June 1941 as a cool and courageous officer capable of taking swift and decisive action in the heat of battle.

While his reputation for bravery in battle grew so did his reputation for brawling. On one occasion he threatened a senior officer, Geoffrey Keyes, who was to win a posthumous VC trying to capture Rommel in November 1941, and his drinking binges while off duty

were already the stuff of legend. One of his fellow commando officers, Lt Gerald Bryan, recalled of Mayne: 'When sober, a gentler, more mild-mannered man you could not wish to meet, but when drunk, or in battle, he was frightening. I'm not saying he was a drunk, but he could drink a bottle of whisky in an evening before he got a glow on.'

One story has it that Stirling recruited Mayne to L Detachment in the summer of 1941 when he was in the glasshouse after striking a senior officer. This is apocryphal. He was actually at the Middle East Commando depot waiting for a posting after the disbandment of Layforce, hoping he might be sent to China to train the Chinese Nationalist Army in how to wage guerrilla warfare against the Japanese.

Mayne accepted Stirling's invitation to join his fledging unit and the pair soon formed a devastating partnership – despite their contrasting personalities. Stirling was at ease in polite society, a man with a ready charm whose charisma normally got him what he wanted. Mayne, though intelligent and thoughtful, was a man of few words. Volatile, aggressive and brusque to the point of downright rudeness, Mayne's imposing physique did most of his talking.

Paddy Mayne oversees a rugby scrum as the SAS relax during their training.

Far East that resulted in supplies destined for Africa being diverted to help in the fight against the Japanese. Rommel launched a counter-attack on 21 January. A week later Benghazi was captured and in early February Tmimi was also in German hands, although that marked the extent of the

BERETS AND WINGS

The first SAS beret was white, but the soldiers privileged to wear it soon discovered it brought with it problems and not prestige. 'When we wore the white berets we were mistaken for Russians and got called names,' recalled Jimmy Storie, one of L Detachment's Originals. 'It was causing so much trouble that they were changed to sand-coloured berets.'

The SAS continued to wear the sand-coloured beret right through 1943 when it was temporarily reconstituted as the Special Raiding Squadron and fought its way from southern Sicily up into Italy. In 1944, however, the SAS acquired Brigade status as an adjunct to the Army Air Corps under the command of Brig Gen Rory McLeod. He instructed both 1SAS and 2SAS to replace the sand-coloured beret with the red airborne headwear, a decision that didn't sit well with desert veterans, particularly Paddy Mayne. He refused to wear the red beret and was still wearing his sand-coloured one at the end of the war.

As well as the cap badge designed by Bob Tait, L Detachment also sported operational wings, which were the creation of Jock Lewes. Designed with a straight edge on top to distinguish them from other airborne units, the wings represented a scarab beetle with a parachute replacing the scarab. The background colours were dark blue and light blue, representing the university colours of Oxford, Lewes' alma mater, and Cambridge, where Stirling had briefly resided.

Every member of L Detachment who successfully undertook parachute training was entitled to wear the wings on the shoulder, and those soldiers who completed three missions were allowed to sport them above their left breast pocket.

Some of the SAS Originals on leave in Cairo: Charlie Cattell, John Byrne, Arthur Phillips, Jimmy Storie and Arthur Warburton.

Axis thrust east. Its front was established on a line running from Gazala on the coast (30 miles west of Tobruk) to Bir Hakeim 50 miles to the south.

Suddenly the desert war transformed from the fluid conflict of the winter months to a static stalemate with Auchinleck consolidating his defensive positions at Gazala and Rommel resupplying his tired and depleted army as he planned his next move. Although the British wouldn't be ready to launch a new offensive for several more months after the hard fighting of the winter, Auchinleck wanted to maintain the pressure on Rommel. He therefore instructed the SAS to attack Axis aerodromes and shipping in and around Benghazi.

Basing themselves at Siwa Oasis, where amid the palm trees lay a sparkling expanse of water known as Cleopatra's Pool in which the men could bathe, the SAS prepared to go into action once again.

They set off in mid-March but only Mayne's party met with success, destroying 15 planes on Berka satellite airfield. Bill Fraser drew a blank at Barce airfield while two new officers, Roy Dodd and Gordon Alston, also failed in their attacks at Slonta and Berka main respectively. Stirling had made an audacious attempt (a mission described by MEHQ as 'hare-brained') to blow up enemy shipping in Benghazi harbour. But having sneaked into the port without detection, the raiders were thwarted by a stormy night that prevented them launching their flimsy canoes into the sea.

Another attempt was made in May 1942, the LRDG once more guiding Stirling's small band of saboteurs across the desert to the outskirts of Benghazi. Again they penetrated the port but again they were foiled in their attempt to sink Axis shipping, this time by a defective valve on the inflatable boat.

Breaking the stalemate

Throughout March and April 1942 Gen Auchinleck was being pressurised by Winston Churchill to break the deadlock in North Africa. The Auk's standoff with Rommel was continuing and the Prime Minister was growing ever more fractious with his general; not only did the British public need some good news, what with the disaster that had befallen their troops in the Far East, where the Japanese had captured Hong Kong, Singapore, Rangoon and Kuala Lumpur in a matter of weeks, but Churchill feared Malta was in danger of falling into German hands, which, as he emphasized in a wire sent to Auchinleck in late April, would be 'a disaster of the first magnitude for the British Empire'.

The locals at Siwa lived parallel but separate lives to the SAS soldiers, although they did sell them dates, figs and chickens to supplement their rations.

The pools at Siwa Oasis were a delight for the soldiers after a hard hot day in the desert.

So anxious was Churchill to prevent Axis forces seizing Malta, strategically crucial to both sides, that he ordered a large convoy to sail for Malta during a moonless period in June in order to keep its defenders supplied. Auchinleck was ordered to go on the offensive to coincide with the convoy, but before he could do so Rommel launched an attack of his own on 26 May. The British defences at first repulsed the German attack, and on 2 June Churchill cabled Auchinleck and Air Marshal Arthur Tedder, Deputy Air Officer Commanding in Chief, Middle East Command, to inform him that two supply convoys would soon be on their way to Malta (from Gibraltar and Alexandria), stating: 'There is no need for me to stress the vital importance of the safe arrival of our convoys ... and I am sure you will both take all steps to enable the air escorts, and particularly the Beaufighters, to be operated from landing-grounds as far west as possible.'

Stirling was summoned to Cairo and told the SAS must launch a series of simultaneous raids against enemy aerodromes in the Benghazi area: every Axis aircraft destroyed would be one less threat to the convoys steaming to Malta.

On 8 June, escorted by a LRDG patrol under the command of Lt the Hon Robin Gurdon, Stirling and 12 men left Siwa bound for the Libyan coast. They travelled in seven LRDG Chevrolet trucks and Stirling's 'Blitz Buggy', a stripped-down Ford V8 staff car that he had appropriated earlier in the year.

Stirling had organised his men into three patrols, one under his command, one under Mayne and the third consisting of Frenchmen led by 29-year-old Lt André Zirnheld, before the war a professor of philosophy. The results were mixed, with Zirnheld's patrol managing to blow up six aircraft, but Mayne and his men were thwarted by the strength of the enemy defences.

It was a similar story for Roger Boutinot, whose patrol under Lt Jacquier, had been tasked with attacking Barce airfield. 'All the lights came on as we approached', he recalled. 'It was so well guarded it was clear they were waiting for us.' Nonetheless, by the end of June the SAS had destroyed at

Initially escorted by the LRDG to targets, in June 1942 the SAS became self-sufficient when it took ownership of some Willys Bantam jeeps.

NIGHT OF JULY 7/8 1941

SAS carry out the first jeep-borne airfield raid

least 27 aircraft (Stirling reduced all tallies by 10 per cent so that he couldn't be accused of exaggerating its success by envious staff officers within MEHQ), 20 to 30 aero engines and 'numerous' fuel dumps.

However, by the end of June Rommel had at last captured Tobruk and advanced to within 65 miles of Alexandria, forcing the LRDG to withdraw from its base at Siwa. Stirling had dashed back to Cairo and received instructions from Auchinleck to concentrate his unit at Qaret Tartura on the north-western edge of the Qattara Depression. From this remote base Stirling 'would try to deliver a simultaneous attack on five or six airfields on the night of July 7th–8th and also blast the coast road' as the Eighth Army counter-attacked.

The 15 jeeps that Stirling took with him when he set off for his new base were escorted by an LRDG patrol commanded by Capt Alistair Timpson, consisting of around 20 vehicles that 'groaned with supplies for a three-week stay in the desert'.

Once the convoy had reached the rendezvous deep in the desert's interior, Stirling outlined the plan of attack to his men. The next night they would raid six targets, the first bombs coordinated to explode simultaneously at 0100 hours. Stirling and Mayne would attack the airfields at Bagush, while Lts Bill Fraser and Augustin Jordan would lead British and French parties to airfields at Fuka, east of Bagush, and a fifth unit would lay waste to Sidi Barrani. Finally, Earl George Jellicoe and Lt Zirnheld would jointly command an Anglo-French raid on the coast road from Fuka to Galal.

Once again the results were mixed. At Sidi Barrani it was discovered that the airfields were used only during the day to bring in supplies on transport planes; Jellicoe and Zirnheld captured 'a few stray prisoners' but encountered no vehicles on the road from Fuka to Galal; the attacks on the landing grounds at Fuka resulted in the destruction of ten aircraft but the mission was deemed to have 'miscarried' because the presence during the lie-up of a large enemy column prevented an adequate reconnaissance of the target.

The first jeep attack

Mayne and Stirling, meanwhile, were having an eventful time at Bagush, as Jellicoe described in his report on the operation:

> Capt. Mayne went on with a small party to make his attack. Normal equipment was carried, each man having one Tommy gun or Colt automatic, two hand grenades, and special [Lewes] bombs. The bombs were placed on the wings of the aircraft and Capt. Mayne came back to report to Major Stirling. He then did the same thing again. Major Stirling had meanwhile been examining the road to see if there was any chance of establishing a road block, but had not made one as he did not think it worthwhile to disclose his position for the sake of an odd truck. When Capt. Mayne had returned for the second time, Major Stirling and he drove on to the aerodrome and destroyed by machine gun fire from their vehicles, a further ten or fourteen aircraft.
>
> Subsequently a reconnaissance showed that in all thirty seven aircraft had been destroyed, mostly C.R. 42s and M.E. 109s. Major Stirling was by this time encountering considerable opposition from M.Gs [machine guns] and 20mm. guns distributed round the landing ground. He therefore withdrew but was unable to resist the temptation to return, to Capt. Mayne's disgust, in order to despatch a few more aircraft!

What Jellicoe's report omitted was an explanation of why Stirling had driven on to the airfield after Mayne's initial foray. The Irishman had destroyed

David Stirling in his Blitz Buggy, a stripped down Ford V8 staff car.

The SAS soon customised their jeeps, installing Brownings, single Vickers and twin Vickers, so that the vehicles boasted awesome firepower.

22 aircraft, but the bombs on a further dozen or so had failed to ignite because, as it was subsequently discovered, the primers were all damp. 'It's enough to break your heart', said Mayne, forlorn at the thought of so many enemy aircraft close at hand and just waiting to be blown up. It was at this moment that Stirling suggested they finish the job with machine gun fire. With Stirling driving his Blitz Buggy and Mayne at the wheel of the jeep, the raiders set off to finish what they had started.

There was no roar of engines or screech of tyres, rather the vehicles approached at a steady pace with the gunners mindful of Stirling's advice to shoot low and aim at the petrol tanks. Johnny Cooper was manning the forward gun on the Blitz Buggy:

> We drove on to the airfield and started firing. He [Stirling] kept to a nice steady pace of about 15 mph and I opened fire at a line of CR 42s that were soon in flames. Unfortunately after three magazines the Vickers had a seizure from overheating … but the damage done to the gun was more than compensated by the devastation caused to the enemy.

So were sown in that raid the seeds for future SAS attacks in the desert. Stirling, Mayne and the other officers must have discussed the potential of jeep attacks in the days following the drive on to the airfield at Bagush, for on 11 July the SAS returned to Fuka's airfields and Lt Bill Fraser, in the words of the operational report, 'decided to drive on to the landing ground [LG 17] and attack with machine guns, as had been recently done by Major Stirling and Capt. Mayne'.

Unfortunately for Fraser, in the process of penetrating the aerodrome's defences 'one of the two jeeps fell into a rifle pit and was extricated with great difficulty under fire'. As the SAS returned fire the machine gun mountings in the second jeep loosened and the attack was aborted.

At Fuka, LG 16, Lt Augustin Jordan led three men towards the airfield, one of whom was Roger Boutinot. 'When we arrived at Fuka there was an electric fence all around the aerodrome', he recalled. As the Frenchmen considered how to surmount this obstacle they were spotted by the sentries, who then fired a red Very light. Jordan, a small austere man with a great intellect (after the war he became France's ambassador to Austria), sprang into action. 'He walked into a tent full of Germans and threw two grenades inside and blew the lot up', remembered Boutinot. With the guards eliminated the Frenchmen set about the aircraft, noting to their relief that there were no guards under each plane, as was increasingly the case in the light of the SAS raids. 'I prepared the bombs, Jordan put them on the plane and the other two kept guard', said Boutinot, who recalled that they adjusted the fuses for just a ten-minute delay.

Paddy Mayne, DSO and three bars, whose idea it was to use jeeps in the desert raids.

The planes were all together, not spaced out, so we went from one to another. Jordan was very calm, always calm. As we were leaving the Germans started firing although I don't think they could see us. That was my first time under fire, it was terrifying at the time but I had volunteered to do it. Martin got shot and lost the top of his thumb, and we destroyed eight planes.

Jordan's party evaded the Germans and returned to their rendezvous with the LRDG with the news of their success. Nonetheless, it had been a close call and once again brought into sharp relief the problems inherent in any attack on foot.

On 12 July, the day after Jordan's attack on Fuka LG 17, there came news that another party of French SAS, commanded by Lt François Martin, had been attacked by Italian Macchi fighter aircraft near Minqar Sida. The LRDG escort had taken the brunt of the strafing and its leader, Lt Robin Gurdon, had died of his wounds.

The death of Gurdon, a popular and above all highly effective officer, was a severe blow to the LRDG and further antagonized its CO, Lieutenant-Colonel Guy Prendergast. In February 1942 he had written to the Brigadier

Some of the dunes of the Great Sand Sea had to be negotiated by vehicles with great care or else serious injuries would occur.

General Staff of the Eighth Army complaining that Stirling was taking 'a big risk' in some of the operations. At the end of May Prendergast wrote in the LRDG diary that the requirements foisted on them by the SAS was 'straining the unit's own resources and personnel'.

Whether Prendergast had any say in Stirling's decision or whether the SAS commander simply decided the time was right for his unit to become self-sufficient isn't known, but on 13 July Stirling returned to Cairo in search of the jeeps required to make the SAS an independent force, having first signalled:

> IMMEDIATE. Willys Bantams great success. Most urgent that twenty five exactly the same type be despatched for modification to fix mounts for twin Vickers guns and sun compass. All gun mountings must be welded, not brazed. We will require six new Ford three tonners, proportionate desert equipment to look after increased scale of operations. Withdrawing force from operations to collect Bantams and three tonners 16th [July]. We return here with smallest delay.

13 JULY 1942

Stirling returns to Cairo to acquire more jeeps for a mass attack

Paddy Mayne went with Stirling, travelling in the heavier vehicles along with the wounded and unfit men who had been behind enemy lines for nearly two weeks. Left behind at Bir el Quseir – they had moved the hideout 25 miles west from Qaret Tartura because of fears they'd been spotted by Italian aircraft – were 23 men who had no clear idea how long Stirling would be gone, only that when he returned he would have a lot more jeeps and a plan to use them in a violent strike against the enemy.

THE PLAN

Back in Cairo Stirling presented himself at HQ Eighth Army whereupon he was issued with Operation Instruction No. 99. It stated:

Formation of a base at Qara Oasis.

You will discuss this with Lieut. Col Prendergast who will forward proposals to Eighth Army Tactical H.Q.

Priorities for Raiding.

The order of priorities is Tank Workshops, tanks, aircraft, water, petrol. You will use your own judgment in assessing the value and reliability of information, importance of target assessed in terms of numbers of tanks, aircraft, etc. and possibilities of successful attack.

Raids by other parties.

Eighth Army H.Q. will, whenever possible, keep you informed of other raiding parties operating in your area, but as these operations may have to be put on at short notice, no guarantee can be given that you will be warned in every case.

Blocking Operations.

In addition to the normal raiding tasks in para. 2 above, you will be prepared for the following operations:-

Operations at Sollum and Halfaya.

One detachment to initiate a traffic block at Sollum. This block will be maintained until a party of Royal Marines has been landed to exploit the situation and maintain the block for 48 hours. As soon as the R.M. party is in position you will hand over to them, and withdraw. You will provide a second detachment to block Halfaya and arrange to keep this block going for 48 hours if possible. The action of this detachment will be co-ordinated with the Sollum Detachment.

A party under Capt. Buck[1] may collaborate with you if it is placed at your disposal by G.H.Q., M.E.

Blocking at Bagush and Gerewla.

---

1   Capt Herbert Buck MC, erstwhile of the Punjab Regiment, commanded the Special Interrogation Group, a unit consisting largely of German Jews who had fled Palestine.

Members of B Squadron, SAS, plan a raid in late 1942. The officer in the middle is the noted desert explorer Wilfred Thesiger, who served briefly in the regiment.

You will prepare to initiate traffic blocks at Bagush and Gerewla. If these operations are approved instructions will be sent to you.

Intercomm.

You will arrange with Lieut. Col. Prendergast that all W/T messages sent by LRDG links reach you as soon as possible.

Stirling must have read Instruction 99 with a mixture of excitement and anger. Section 2 would have put a smile on his face – the go-ahead to attack tanks and aircraft – but his heart must have sunk when he read that the SAS might be required to act as blocking troops to the Royal Marines (this idea was shelved by the GHQ's Deputy Director of Military Intelligence because 'handing over' was deemed too impractical) or work with Capt Buck's Special Interrogation Group.

Following recent events at Fuka and Bagush, Stirling was clearer than ever in his mind that a mass jeep attack would provide the SAS with a means of hitting the enemy again, both physically and mentally. As he told his biographer, Alan Hoe, nearly 50 years later: 'It was not change for change's sake … if we could keep them guessing and use a variety of tactics in such a

manner that they never knew what was coming where, and how it was being delivered, we could sow real confusion in the rear.'

The problem was that Eighth Army HQ took a narrow view of the SAS. With Rommel just 65 miles from Alexandria it had plenty more pressing concerns in July 1942 than the feelings of Stirling. As Stirling told his biographer:

> MEHQ still insisted on labelling us as saboteurs. Damn it, we were not saboteurs, we were a strategically effective force which could use sabotage as a tactic if the task called for it … the SAS was based on maximum achievement for minimum cost; who could possibly argue with that? I don't believe that even Auchinleck, who had helped me so much, had wholly grasped the awesome potential of the SAS as a permanent unit.

Auchinleck, at least, still valued the SAS even if, as Stirling stated, his imagination failed to understand their full potential. But other staff officers in MEHQ disliked the SAS and their leader, believing that they were a renegade unit that should be absorbed by a more structured organisation such as the Special Operations Executive (SOE).

The antipathy was mutual. Stirling referred in private to junior staff officers as 'fossilised shit' and it was a constant battle with headquarters to get the supplies he wanted. It was Stirling's belief that by pulling off a 'spectacular', such as a mass jeep raid on an enemy airfield, he would once and for all silence his enemies within MEHQ.

In order to lay the groundwork for such a raid, Stirling highlighted the advantages of using jeeps in a paper he submitted to Eighth Army Headquarters. In it he stated:

> Attacks on landing ground have never before taken place when the moon was full; and the first attack at least would have the advantage of surprise.
>
> The enemy's tendency during periods of moonlight was to scatter aircraft over a number of landing grounds in order to minimise the effects of R.A.F bombing. They

Reconnaissance photographs of an Axis desert airfield. They were used by the SAS to plan one of their many raids.

were too numerous to be adequately defended, and successful attacks would result either in a concentration of aircraft on a few well defended landing grounds, which would render them more vulnerable to bombing, or of tying up much needed troops by strengthening the defence of a large number of them.

A 'mass attack' would nullify the value of sentries on individual aircraft (the enemy's normal custom) and would necessitate perimeter defence, which past experience has shown to be comparatively easy to penetrate by 'stealth'. Thus the alternative employment of two methods of attack – either by a small party on foot reaching its objective without being observed, or by a 'mass' attack in vehicles – should leave the enemy hesitating between the two methods of defence. A combination of perimeter defence with sentries on individual aircraft would be the most uneconomical in men.

The psychological effect of successful attacks should increase the enemy's nervousness about the defence of his extended lines of communication.

Waiting in the desert

As Stirling careered around Cairo, gathering supplies and support, back in the desert the men he had left behind were enduring the full unforgiving force of the Libyan Desert.

On 13 July Capt Nick Wilder, the rugged and resourceful commander of the LRDG's T Patrol – comprised of New Zealanders – wrote in the unit's diary: 'Major Stirling left for Cairo, leaving T Patrol and twenty paratroops behind. O.C. T Patrol put in charge (Wilder) of party. At 1800 hrs eight men from T patrol set off to watch main road and barrel route between Sidi Haneish and Fuka under corporal [Merlyn] Craw.'

Craw was a farmer from the north island of New Zealand, a tough man typical of his countrymen. For the next few days T Patrol carried out road watches on the route from Qara to Matruh, noting down all they saw of enemy transport.

The 20 soldiers of the SAS had received no orders from Stirling before he departed for Cairo other than sit and wait for his return. With their hideout at Bir el Quseir only 50 miles from the nearest Axis airfields, planes often passed overhead, so the soldiers were obliged to spend most of the day hidden 'in the side of the long, fifty-foot high escarpment, like rabbits in a warren'. The jeeps and trucks had been concealed in the crevices of the escarpment and camouflaged with nets and scrubs.

'We were under the continual apprehension that the enemy would discover our hideout by aircraft or by ground patrols,' recalled Lt Carol Mather, who had joined the SAS from the Welsh Guards and Layforce. 'There were so many tracks leading from all directions to our escarpment and running along the foot of the cliff itself that we had to take every precaution' (Carol Mather papers, IWM). Mather and another officer, Lt Stephen Hastings, organised sentry duty atop a pimple on the escarpment. 'From this point we could get a view of all the surrounding country,' said Mather. 'And we would search round and round with our glasses over the barren landscape, staring for minutes on end at dust clouds and vehicles which seemed to be making our way, only to disperse in mirages.'

Dick Holmes and Duggie Pomford joined the SAS in the late summer of 1942, later serving in the SBS.

Hastings had only recently joined L Detachment, having fought with the Scots Guards in the desert war, and he was still enjoying the contrast between his new unit and his former regiment. 'We were a wild-looking lot,' he recalled in his autobiography, *The Drums of Memory*. 'Most wore a pair of shorts, sandals or boots with rubber soles and either bush hats or big khaki handkerchiefs over their heads like the Bedouin. We all had beards.'

Among the SAS soldiers were three French officers – Augustin Jordan, François Martin and André Zirnheld – who lived among their British comrades. The LRDG Kiwis kept themselves to themselves, burrowing into another part of the escarpment, while they rested between road watches.

The SAS envied the LRDG their tasks, wishing they had some way of breaking the monotony. Capt Malcolm Pleydell, L Detachment's medical officer, wrote that 'waiting is far worse than being employed on active operations'. Marooned in their desert hideout, fearful that they could be discovered by the enemy at any moment, Pleydell described their existence as 'real anguish and bleak loneliness'. The boredom brought with it other problems – namely, water consumption. On operations soldiers often forgot their thirst in the excitement, but counting every second of every hour at Bir el Quseir they were as plagued by thirst as they were by flies.

Men sought solace in one another, palling up with their comrades to help pass the dragging, despondent hours. 'In the early morning Steve and I would walk down … to our daytime cave near the cook-house,' recalled Mather. 'Here we would spend the remainder of the day. It was a long and low grotto with a floor of soft, white sand, at one end a great lip curved over, touching the ground and forming a cool enclosed space.'

Here the pair sheltered from the sun, reading one of the three paperbacks they had with them – *The Virginians*, *Seven Pillars of Wisdom* and *For Whom the Bell Tolls* – or engaged in conversation. One of their favourite topics was the marine fossils and shells embedded in the rock above their heads, the pair discussing how and when they got to be there.

Another soldier, Sgt Jim Almonds, one of L Detachment's original members from 12 months earlier, one morning discovered more evidence of their hideout's rich history. Spotting some pottery fragments among the escarpment he took them to Malcolm Pleydell. There were enough fragments to piece together a 'beautifully symmetrical handle' of a vase that Pleydell reckoned came from the Greek or Roman periods (Pleydell later presented the fragments to the curator of the Museum of Cairo who dated the vase to between 100 and 300 BC).

Pleydell also found plenty of marine fossils printed on the rocks of their hideout and at night, after their supper of bully beef mixed with biscuit and dried vegetables, he would lie on his back and study the stars overhead. The doctor wrote of the stars:

> They were wise in their old age, wise, and probably very cynical as they watched the futile efforts of mankind. For, over two thousand years ago, they had seen the army of Cambyses march to its unknown fate.[2] They had seen the Romans and Carthaginians locked in pitiless battle. They had looked down upon the Turks as they strove to hold the mastery of the desert. They had watched the childish brutality of the Italians as they tortured and drove the Senussi from one oasis to another. They had seen us warring in the desert twenty years ago, and now here we were back at it again. In a fraction of a second in the history of time, they had watched these little dramas of puny man – each, in turn, had strutted across the sandy stage and held it for a fleeting instant – and then the dust had blown over in its caressing forgetfulness, his traces had been concealed and his ways had become just a memory.

On 21 July, a week after Stirling and Mayne had left for Cairo, there was still no sign of them and the men at Bir el Quseir began to fret quietly. Lookouts posted on top of the escarpment scanned the horizon but each time a comrade called up from below if they could see something the same negative reply came back. On the afternoon of the ninth day both food and

2   Legend has it that Cambyses, son of Cyrus the Great, despatched 50,000 soldiers from Thebes to destroy the oracle at the Temple of Amun at Siwa in 525 BC. But during its march the Persian Army was swallowed up by a huge sandstorm. As no trace has ever been found of the army it is in all probability nothing more than a myth.

Grub's up! An LRDG patrol waits for its supper at the end of the day.

water were running low (they were now existing on a mug and a half of water a day per man), and Hastings, Mather and Pleydell started to discuss their options. Then, around 1600 hours on 23 July, they heard the sentry cry: 'There's vehicles in sight, sir, coming from the east!'

Everyone scrambled to the escarpment and the officers held their field glasses to their faces and peered in the direction the sentry pointed. 'Far away in the shimmering mirage which constituted our horizon we could see several little black dots,' recalled Hastings. 'Their shape kept changing; now some appeared elongated as if reflected in a bent mirror; two would merge into one and then part again. They were certainly moving.'

The question that neither Hastings nor anyone else perched on top of the escarpment knew was, were the vehicles friend or foe? The Bren gun was brought up from a cave and the soldiers cocked their weapons. 'The minutes ticked by,' said Hastings, 'and then suddenly they emerged from the mirage, quite close and recognizable – jeeps and several 30cwt trucks. It was the column from Cairo.'

Capt Nick Wilder marked the event with a laconic entry in the LRDG diary: '23/7: Major Stirling returned from Cairo.'

The jeeps arrive

Stirling was at the head of a 20-strong column of jeeps, 'all of them bristling with Vickers K guns', while the 30cwt trucks mentioned by Hastings were weighed down with supplies. A week earlier, at the request of Stirling,

Capt Ken Lazarus of the LRDG had set out from Cairo with four trucks from the unit's Heavy Section. Crossing the Qattara Depression, they deposited the supplies as arranged near the former hideout at Qaret Tartura. Stirling's convoy had then collected them en route to the new base. The supplies included 1,500 gallons of petrol, 30 gallons M.220 oil, 30 gallons C.600 oil, 300 hand grenades, 5,000 incendiary bullets and an unspecified quantity of tea, sugar and powdered milk.

Welcome as the LRDG supplies were, the 20 or so bearded, burnt and famished men at Bir el Quseir were far more delighted to receive the supplies harvested by Stirling in Cairo. These included 'tobacco, rum, new pipes, Turkish Delight and a pint jar of Eau de Cologne'. The return of Stirling was just the tonic the men needed. Hastings reminisced that 'fresh fires flickered up that evening in the failing light … three brews of tea with rum and cigarettes afterwards.'

There were now about 50 men in total at the hideout and after supper Stirling gathered his officers around him. First they toasted his return with a wee drop of whisky, then Stirling got down to business. One item on the agenda was the introduction of some new faces, men who had come up from Cairo at the invitation of Stirling. Carol Mather remembered:

Sandy Scratchley, Chris Bailey and David Russell had come up with the new party, also another RAF officer to replace David Rawnsley. His name was Pike and he was an Australian who had just come off flying duties to help us in being supplied by the air. He was young, well-built and good looking. He had charm and great enthusiasm, and he was intrigued by everything about us – our beards, our jeeps and the way we lived

The LRDG Heavy Section, some of whom are seen here, were responsible for bringing supplies from Cairo to the SAS desert bases.

23 JULY 1942

Stirling returns from Cairo with more jeeps and supplies

Paddy Mayne, far right, and a group of SAS soldiers relax between raids.

and worked … Chris Bailey had transferred from the Cyprus company of the 4th Hussars and had spent over a year at Eighth Army HQ. Before the war he had kept an inn on Cyprus, which was renowned for its kitchen.

David Russell had recently arrived in Egypt with a Scots Guard draft. He was a wild and independent character, who enjoyed everything he did, who demanded complete obedience from soldiers, but who didn't necessarily give it to his superiors – in this way he wasn't popular with everybody.

Stirling also introduced the unit's new navigator, Sgt Mike Sadler, formerly of the Rhodesian patrol of the LRDG, a man whose directional savvy had prompted Stirling to prise him from one special forces unit to drop into another. 'I think Stirling got the jeeps first but hadn't the means to navigate so that's when he talent spotted me, if that's the word, having seen me on early ops with the LRDG,' recalls Sadler.

As the navigator for the Rhodesian patrol, Sadler had guided Paddy Mayne to Tamet airfield in December 1941 and subsequently worked with the SAS on other raids behind enemy lines. 'Stirling had a very good social manner and also had a compelling personality,' says Sadler. 'He could talk you into anything, but he didn't have to do much talking… He managed to make one feel you were the only person who could possibly do it, that kind of effect, but I also slightly felt he was thinking of something else at the same time.'

Even though Sadler had got Mayne to Tamet six months earlier, he knew less about the Irishman than he did Stirling. Nonetheless, he had seen enough of Mayne to know that 'Paddy felt his true vocation in war; he was well suited to war and he enjoyed it … I don't think he fancied the idea of being shot more than anyone else but he had a very good control of himself.' As for comparing and contrasting the two men, Sadler said:

I always felt that the great difference between him and Paddy on an op was that Paddy was focused on the operation and knew everything that everybody was doing and where they were. David tended to be thinking ahead; next time we'll need some other equipment and we could do it differently. I navigated him on a road we did up on a coast road somewhere, can't remember where exactly, but we ran into a German laager that we shot up and pulled down some telegraph poles. There was a bit of fire from the Germans but once we got out of range of that he said 'oh you drive now, Mike' (at that stage I had been doing the machine gunning as well as the navigating) and he got into the other seat and curled up asleep. I was left with the task of finding the way back but he was rather like that. He was the strategic fellow, he had the ideas and was always thinking of improvements to make. (Author interview, 2003)

The airfield at Sidi Haneish

But the main topic of discussion that night was the mass jeep raid that had been fermenting in Stirling's mind for the past ten days. Malcolm Pleydell recalled that Stirling explained first why the change in tactic was needed before outlining his plan. Using jeeps they would rely 'on the sheer weight of firepower to overcome any defence that the enemy guards might muster', their 'machine-guns firing in tight concentration as the cars drove this way and that across the aerodrome'.

As for the target, Stirling unfurled his map and pointed to Sidi Haneish, a hitherto unmolested airfield approximately 30 miles east-south-east of Mersa Matruh and around 50 miles north of their hideout. Also known as

Some of the SAS in the summer of 1942. The unit's medical officer, Malcolm Pleydell, is standing second from the right in the middle.

MIKE SADLER – KING OF THE COMPASS

Born in February 1920 in London, Mike Sadler grew up in the south-west of England and went to prep school in Cirencester. One of his teachers enthralled the young Sadler with 'great stories about Africa and the tigers' and shortly after his 17th birthday he emigrated to Rhodesia to become a farmer. On the outbreak of war, Sadler joined a Rhodesian artillery battery but differences of opinion with his commanding officer – and the tedium of his existence – made him look elsewhere for excitement. A chance encounter with some members of the Rhodesian patrol of the LRDG while on leave in Cairo led Sadler to join the unit in the autumn of 1941. After a little over six months' service with the LRDG, Sadler was headhunted by Stirling and he remained with the SAS until the end of the war, rising to the rank of Captain. He received his commission from Stirling in unusual circumstances. 'When we were in Cairo he said, "I want you to be an officer, go and buy some pips." So I went down one of the bazaars and bought some.' A few weeks later Sadler accompanied Stirling as he harried the retreating Germans into Tunisia. To add to the excitement, their unit was probably the first from the Eighth Army to link up with the First Army, which was advancing east after the landings in November in Morocco and Algeria as part of Operation *Torch*.

Unfortunately Stirling's patrol was detected by the Germans and everyone except Sadler, Johnny Cooper and a French soldier called Freddie Taxis were captured. 'For the next three days and four nights we walked from east to west with great salt lakes to one side,' says Sadler of their escape. 'Fortunately I knew the lay of the land and how to navigate but it was still pretty rugged going. We managed to replenish the goatskin [water bottle] with some brackish water from a well and we had a few dates for food to keep us going but that was it.'

Finally, they reached Free French lines at Tozeur in south-west Tunisia, where they were warmly welcomed. But that all changed when they were handed over to the Americans and driven the 200km to Tebessa under suspicion of being Fifth Columnists. 'We were followed by a jeep load of guards in case we made a break for it, and also a jeep load of pressmen,' recalled Sadler. 'Then when they had checked up on us we were issued with US Lieutenant uniforms and we were OK after that ... there was a bit of a fuss made about the fact we were the Eighth Army meeting the First Army. My local paper in Gloucestershire had an article headed 'Sheepscombe Man in Desert Odyssey'. I think we were the first, unofficially, to get through and make the link.'

Mike Sadler, pictured here at the wheel of a jeep in France, August 1944, was a brilliant navigator who guided the SAS to Sidi Haneish.

Landing Grounds 12/13, it was regularly used by Axis aircraft and, in the words of Jim Almonds, 'just begging' to be hit.

The following day, 24 July, was one of theory. Stirling had the men assembled and explained in minute detail how the raid would unfold. Eighteen jeeps would participate in the attack, travelling to the target under cover of darkness on the 26th. As they approached Sidi Haneish from the south they would form a line abreast and 'on a signal from him they would open up with a spectacular display of tracer bullets to silence the defences and give an impression of great strength'. With the enemy numbed by SAS firepower, Stirling explained that he would then fire two green Very lights, the signal for the jeeps to adopt a new formation; his jeep would be the tip of the attack with two more vehicles either side. Then on each flank would be a column of seven jeeps, spaced five yards apart, the guns of the left-hand column firing outwards and likewise the weapons of the right-hand column. The three vehicles that joined the 'square' would 'move between the two rows of planes, with the guns of the three leading jeeps firing ahead at the defences'. Each jeep was armed with four Vickers K machine guns each with a rate of fire of nearly 1,200 rounds a minute; a twin Vickers on a steel upright in the front passenger seat and another twin Vickers at the right-hand side in the rear.'

The 18th jeep, containing Mike Sadler, would not take part in the attack but instead would drive to the south-east corner of the airfield ready to pick up men in the event of jeeps being incapacitated for any reason.

Meanwhile, Capt Nick Wilder's LRDG patrol, having set off with the SAS raiding party, would break off, and engage any defences west of Sidi Haneish while the attack was launched as a diversion. They would then 'beat up any transport or enemy concentrations to the north west of the LG [Landing Ground].'

Stirling used a stick to draw the formation in the sand and then informed the men that the following night, 25 July, they would hold a full dress rehearsal to allow everyone to familiarize themselves with their role in the raid. After all, he said, 'it was like learning a dance routine'.

Until then, concluded Stirling, they would drive half a mile or so from the escarpment and practise their formation until he was happy each driver knew what he had to do. 'First attempts were muddled,' admitted Stephen Hastings. 'But eventually distances and drill were more or less perfected and the idea of the jeep charge became reality.'

Everyone found the dress rehearsal an almost surreal experience, driving around the desert, hundreds of miles inside enemy territory. 'The rehearsal was one of the more bizarre moments of the war for me,' recalled Johnny Cooper, 'firing thousands of rounds deep behind enemy lines in preparation for a raid the following night.'

Pleydell would not be going on the raid, instead remaining at the hideout ready to treat the wounded on their return, but as a consolation Paddy Mayne allowed him to sit in his jeep during the practice. Squeezing between Mayne and the front gunner, with the rear gunner taking up most of the room behind, Pleydell had practically the best seat in the house for the dress rehearsal, which was conducted a few miles from their hideout.

'David [Stirling] was in the centre of the front row, while we were out on the right flank of the square,' recalled Pleydell. 'At the given command we moved off across the scrub-scattered plain, little dark shadows lurching and bumping, with the drivers trying hard to maintain their correct position.'

The drivers discovered that keeping close formation at night was infinitely more challenging then during the day. Suddenly Stirling fired the first of his Very lights, said Pleydell, 'throwing us all into a garishly green electrical sort of relief'. That was the signal for the gunners to join the fray.

24 JULY 1942

Stirling explains the plan for the Sidi Haneish raid

25 JULY 1942

SAS carry out a full-scale, live-fire rehearsal of the raid

'Up the Blue' was the SAS slang for desert operations. Here three men take a break in December 1942.

'Our magazines contained a mixture of incendiary, ball and armour piercing and tracer bullets,' wrote Carol Mather. 'We practised forming into line abreast and line astern, firing on the green Very signal from David's jeep and following exactly in the tracks of the leaders. Every gun fired outwards and as I was driving and at the end of the left hand column, my front gun fired across my face and my rear gun behind my head so it was important to sit very still and not to lean backwards or forwards.'

Pleydell was almost overwhelmed by the violence of the four Vickers K machine guns in Mayne's jeep, which shook 'with each shuddering burst'. The noise was deafening and the men laughed at the sight of the pyrotechnics so deep behind the enemy lines. 'We had a run-in of about 50 miles to Sidi Haneish and it was perfectly safe,' reflected Sadler of the practice. 'Really, the chances of anyone being within 20 or 30 miles of us was very remote.'

When Stirling was satisfied each jeep could change position and direction without a problem, he called an end to the rehearsal. On their return to the escarpment Pleydell was privy to Paddy Mayne's understated style of leadership.

'What direction are we driving in?' he suddenly said, turning to the front gunner.

The man stared at the stars, trying to figure out which star was which. At length he replied:

'North-east, I should say, sir.'

'Ha!' exclaimed Mayne. 'You wouldn't get far if you had to walk back.'

Changing gear, Mayne cast a sideways glance at his gunner and said quietly: 'Mind you're certain of your direction by tomorrow night.'

Pleydell fell asleep that night to the sound of George Jellicoe and Sandy Scratchley (a jockey before the war, described by a contemporary as 'a famous hurdle race amateur jockey, the best of his time, a man of great common sense') laughing as they reflected on the dress rehearsal.

The next morning the men were up early, wrapped up warm against the cold and relieved that for the time being at least they were not plagued by the flies that arrived with the midday sun.

Mather likened the activity on the morning of 26 July to:

the gold mining scene from the Seven Dwarves. There was much hammering and singing as new wheels and tyres were fitted, the Vickers guns were stripped and cleaned, magazines loaded, engines taken down and explosives made up. At one end two 4 gallon petrol cans containing bully stew were simmering over a large fire, at the other end David [Stirling] poring over maps and figures. Paddy [Mayne] fast asleep and unrecognisable entwined under a large mosquito net with his head under one jeep and his feet under another. George [Jellicoe] with a great tin of acid drops in front of him calmly working out the impossible problem of how much stuff we would want and how much we had got.

Men were pleased to be busy; it meant that thoughts of the raid were kept in the back of their minds. Nonetheless, recalled Johnny Cooper: 'I think everyone felt a little bit of fear. But it was more eager anticipation – no one liked hanging around – and we had a desire to get on with it. We checked and rechecked our guns, the jeeps, and loaded the drums in the right order – one tracer, one armour-piercing and one incendiary.'

Mike Sadler, meanwhile, made sure of the route on the map. For him there would not be the stress of driving on to the airfield to shoot up the aircraft; rather he faced anxiety of a different kind. 'There was a certain amount of pressure [as navigator] because there was always the worry you wouldn't pull it off,' he said. 'There was somehow a lot of pressure on that one [Sidi Haneish] because it was a big party and it had a lot of key folk on it.'

Since he had arrived from Cairo a few days earlier, Sadler had got to know some of his new comrades better, besides Stirling and Mayne. Jellicoe he called 'a great man', Pleydell 'a good doctor' and David Russell 'wild and self-confident ... mad but a nice chap'. As for his fellow NCOs, Sadler took

THE ROAD TO SIDI HANEISH

THE WESTERN DESERT, JULY 1942

▼ EVENTS

1. 7–8 July: David Stirling and Paddy Mayne attack Bagush airfield using vehicles instead of going in on foot.

2. 11 July: Inspired by the actions of his CO, Lt Bill Fraser drives onto Fuka airfield.

3. 16 July: David Stirling returns to Cairo to collect a consignment of more Willys Bantam jeeps.

4. 23 July: Stirling arrives at Bir el Quseir with supplies, men and the jeeps.

5. 25 July: The raiders stage a full dress rehearsal practising the raid manoeuvres in their jeeps.

6. 26/27 July: Stirling and the SAS in 18 jeeps attack Sidi Haneish landing strip.

7. 27–29 July: The raiders split after the attack and make their way back to their base at Bir el Quseir 'west of the big track' that ran from the coast to Qara.

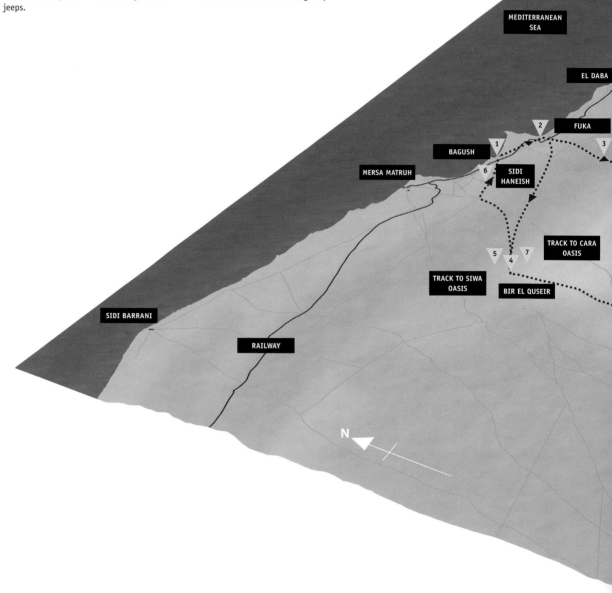

MEDITERRANEAN SEA

EL DABA

FUKA

BAGUSH

MERSA MATRUH

SIDI HANEISH

TRACK TO CARA OASIS

TRACK TO SIWA OASIS

BIR EL QUSEIR

SIDI BARRANI

RAILWAY

N

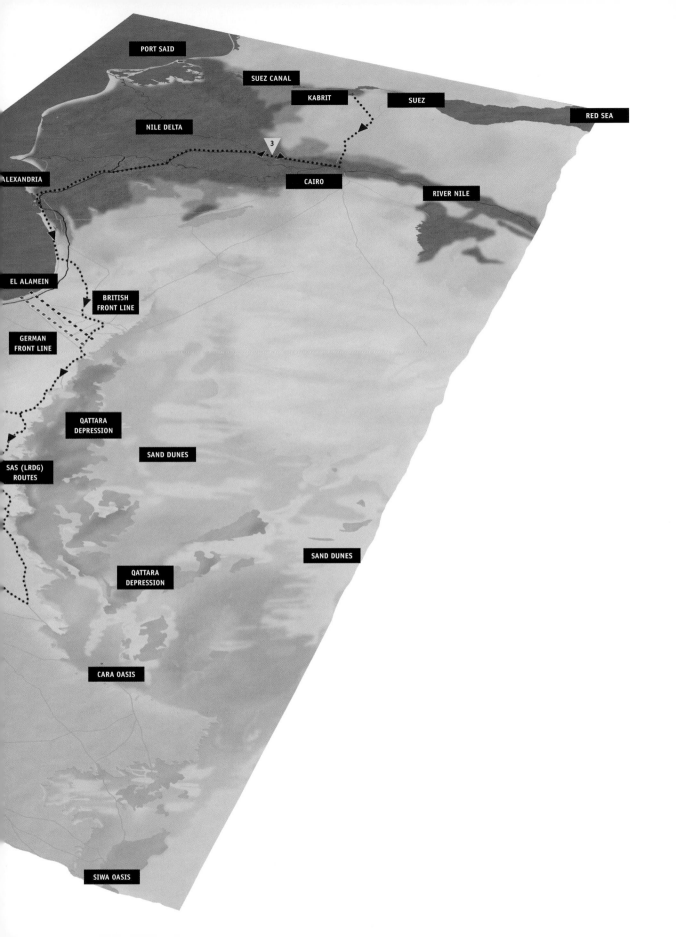

Some of the SAS Originals, including Reg Seekings (front) and Johnny Cooper (far right), both of whom took part in the Sidi Haneish raid.

an instant shine to the inseparable pair of Johnny Cooper and Reg Seekings, both sergeants. 'Reg and Johnny came from very different backgrounds,' recalled Sadler. 'Johnny was better educated and he was a "warrior"; he always wanted to be a soldier. You could sit down and have a chat with Reg but he was a slightly buttoned-up sort of chap.'

Seekings, who thought Sadler looked like a 'university professor', was a hard man who had already won the Distinguished Conduct Medal in the desert campaign. The citation describes how 'This NCO has taken part in 10 raids. He has himself destroyed over 15 aircraft and by virtue of his accuracy with a tommy-gun at night, and through a complete disregard for his personal safety, has killed at least 10 of the enemy.'

Born in the Cambridgeshire Fens in 1920, Seekings, along with Sgt Maj Pat Riley, were the only men in the regiment that Paddy Mayne knew to leave well alone, even when drunk. 'I never had any trouble with him [Mayne] when drinking, nor [did] Pat Riley, because we weren't worried about his size and we both had the confidence we could deal with him,' reflected Seekings, a brilliant amateur boxer before the war. 'And Paddy respected us for that so there was no problem.'

Sadler was right in his description of Seekings as 'buttoned-up'. Like Mayne, Seekings was socially awkward, partly because of his rural upbringing and partly because of his accent. 'The first time I went to London the Cockneys laughed at me because I talked slowly, like Fenmen,' said Seekings. 'But I said "Yeah, maybe, but we think a lot and if there's something we don't understand do you know what we do, and he said no and I said we hit it, and we hit it bloody hard, so watch it, mate".'

Nonetheless, despite his gruff exterior, underneath Seekings was shrewd and perceptive, and surprisingly sympathetic to those less ruthless than himself. 'Battle and fighting more or less face to face can be a bloody terrifying prospect for some people,' he said. 'I was good at it and I suppose to a certain extent I enjoyed it but it's not everyone's cup of tea. At one time yes I enjoyed the killing. I used to fret if a job was cancelled and I enjoyed the adrenaline rush. I was scared but I would have gone into action every day if I could.'

Johnny Cooper was the social opposite of Seekings, a man at ease in all company and a hit with the ladies who fell for his looks, wit and charm. The youngest soldier among the Originals, Cooper celebrated his 20th birthday in June 1942 and was known to Stirling as 'Young Cooper'. Brought up in a middle-class family in Leicestershire, Cooper was an excellent sportsman and an enthusiastic actor (in a Wyggeston Grammar School play he had played Robin Hood to another boy's Maid Marian – the 'boy' being a young Richard Attenborough), but he was also a skilled soldier, a former Scots Guardsman who had endured the debacle of Layforce.

He and Seekings may have had contrasting personalities but they hit it off from the moment they joined the SAS in the summer of 1941, even if Seekings did sometimes have to endure the more exuberant side of his friend during nights out in Cairo. 'I did have a habit of singing once I'd had a few beers, I couldn't help it,' recalled Cooper. 'Poor old Reg was very tolerant, although before we'd go out he'd often ask me not to start singing. But I think perhaps he secretly liked hearing me sing!'

THE RAID

As 26 July wore on and the men finished fitting tyres and wheels and stripping and cleaning weapons and checking, there was nothing left to do but sit and wait for sundown. That was the worst time of all, when a man had time to think. 'I tried to sleep,' admitted Stephen Hastings, 'but lay wondering what it would be like.'

The dress rehearsal had gone as well as could have been expected, but it was easy to pull it off in practice when there was no one trying to kill you from a few yards away. 'What about the defenders,' mused Hastings. 'Would they be dug in? Was there any wire? With luck we should have surprise on our side. The danger could be when the planes came to look for us.'

Hastings was a relative newcomer to this form of warfare, but for an old hand like Sadler, it was exactly this threat that worried him most on each raid. 'Going on an operation, it wasn't the raid itself you worried about,' recalled Sadler. 'It was how the hell were we going to get away afterwards because the Germans were like bees in chasing us.'

As dusk approached and the shadows grew across the escarpment, the raiders began to rouse from their slumber and prepare for the off. Each jeep comprised an officer or NCO behind the wheel with a front and rear gunner. Johnny Cooper and Reg Seekings were in the lead jeep with Stirling. 'Because of his height and his quiet self-confidence he could appear quite intimidating but he wasn't a bawling leader,' said Cooper of Stirling. 'He talked to you, not at you, and he usually gave orders in a very polite fashion. His charisma was overpowering and we followed him everywhere.'

As the men clambered into the vehicles, the drivers revved their engines up and down and adjusted the goggles they wore to protect their eyes from the dust. They were well wrapped up for the evening, when the temperature would often drop below zero, wearing their battledress under their overcoats. Some were bareheaded, some wore woollen cap comforters and one or two had their own idiosyncratic sense of style. Carol Mather had in his jeep Cpl Bob Lilley, a Black Countryman who had joined the Coldstream Guards

before distinguishing himself during the siege of Tobruk while serving with Layforce. 'Lilley wore a headcloth tied in pirate fashion round his head and a long drooping moustache and a thick beard,' recalled Mather. His other gunner was 28-year-old Cpl David Lambie, 'a steady and uncomplaining man' who before the war had been a shunter for the London, Midland and Scottish Railway Company in Ayr harbour, Scotland.

Among the 18 jeeps three were comprised solely of Frenchmen, the vehicles driven by Augustin Jordan, François Martin and André Zirnheld. Also present in their own LRDG vehicles were Capt Nick Wilder's T Patrol. He noted in his diary that it was 1800 hours when the convoy began driving carefully away from Bir el Quseir.

'One by one we pulled out,' recalled Hastings, 'bumping through the soft, churned-up sand at the foot of the escarpment, guns rattling and swinging on their mountings, out on to the firm desert behind.'

Malcolm Pleydell and the handful of men left behind waved them off and then watched them disappear from sight, 'a long line of vicious looking jeeps, each with its attendant plume of dust, standing out sharply against the evening sky'.

Pleydell admitted that the escarpment felt lonely and empty after their departure, but there was scant time to succumb to melancholy. 'We, who were left behind, set to work in tidying up the place and camouflaging the remaining vehicles and off-loading stores more carefully than ever, for we expected considerable attention from aircraft on the following day.'

A deadly convoy

For the first 45 minutes there was still enough light to see where the raiders were headed and the convoy travelled at around 20mph over flat shingle or

An SAS patrol looks to head 'up the Blue'. Note the sand channels stacked on the bonnet to help extract the wheels from deep sand, and also the water condenser on the vehicle's radiator grill.

The SAS wore more or less what they wanted behind the lines in the desert, with leather jerkins particularly popular to combat the cold of the nights.

hard sand. There were one or two small escarpments to negotiate, but progress was good and spirits were high. 'We kept in no particular formation,' said Hastings, 'and the drivers just picked their own way a little to right or left of the man in front and followed his dust.'

The billowing dust precluded conversation so the men were left alone with their thoughts as they moved slowly towards their target. At 1845 hours, in the last vestiges of light, they spotted the Siwa track up ahead. Stirling called a halt and, as one by one the vehicles stopped, he summoned Mike Sadler to the front of the convoy.

Sadler, as chief navigator, was at the rear with Johnny Cooper navigating for Stirling in the front of the column on the bearing given to him at the outset by Sadler. 'The night was relatively bright with a quarter-moon and a fair amount of patchy cloud,' recalled Cooper. 'I navigated using low clouds and a prismatic compass held in my lap.'

Once Sadler had made his way up to Stirling he was asked to fix up his theodolite and take a shot to check their direction. As he did so the men around him smoked and talked, making the most of the break.

Sadler told Stirling they were bang on course, still heading on a 60-degree bearing towards the Qara to Matruh road. Capt Wilder checked the bearing and then shook hands with Stirling, wishing him well. This was the moment they parted company, with the LRDG continuing north while the SAS raiding party turned to the north-east. Hastings looked towards where they were headed. 'Before us, to the north-east, the horizon showed sharp and black, it could have been a range of mountains 20 miles off or a ridge 20 yards away. About us glowed a sea of dull unearthly silver, broken by shadows and the black masses of rocks and ridges ... we moved off east of north and close together.'

Now the driving became harder as the terrain got bumpier and the escarpments grew sharper. Sadler had to concentrate even harder on keeping them all on the right bearing. In the day Sadler navigated using a sun compass, but that wasn't possible at night.

Sadler reflected:

One of the essential things was not to let doubt creep into your mind. You had to be
confident because it was awfully easy, especially at night, when you could easily start
to feel you were going wrong and you should be further to the left or to the right. It
was rather easy to give way to that feeling if you weren't confident. I think I was fairly
rigid about sticking to what I'd worked out, the bearings and the rest of it, and not
allowing those doubts to creep in at night.

At night Sadler had no alternative but to use a magnetic compass, which
in his case was a liquid aircraft compass. 'You couldn't rely on the bearing
in the vehicle as there was so much local influence in the dynamo, load,
and all the metallic things but you could use the compass to tell if you were
going in the right direction or not,' he explained.

The difficulty was, of course, that with every obstacle they encountered
they were compelled to slightly change direction and Sadler had to ensure
they didn't stray off the bearing in the darkness. 'Because you had to
change course for some reason or other, you'd stop and get out and check
and record the bearing,' he said. 'I don't think one was ever far out but I
could see that if you lost confidence in what you'd written down you
would then start guessing but I tried not to do that.'

As the night of 26 July wore on Sadler's skills as a navigator were tested
to the full. At one point, recalled Hastings, they were confronted with a
cliff that appeared insurmountable. Stirling sent out two jeeps to find a
way over the obstacle and they returned with the news that there was a
route round the cliff a quarter of a mile away. The route was in fact a steep
wadi (a gulley or dry river bed in the desert) that skirted around the cliff.

The interior of the Western
Desert was vast, forbidding
and frightening to the Axis
forces, who rarely ventured
too far from the coast in
search of the SAS raiders.

THE SUN COMPASS

Invented by Ralph Bagnold, founder of the LRDG, the sun compass was really a miniature sundial with a white disc on which were a series of marks. Protruding from the centre of the disc was a small needle and it was possible to navigate from the shadow cast on the disc from the needle at any given time of day. Bagnold had hit upon the idea during his travels through the Libyan Desert in the 1920s when he found the traditional magnetic compass was adversely influenced by the metal of the vehicles he was travelling in.

'The first jeep got about halfway up, hit a rock and slithered to the bottom,' recalled Hastings. 'There was a grinding of gears as the drivers reached for the booster. The next car made it, engine racing, and one by one we crashed and bounced up the slope and on through the night like a pack of mechanized wolves.'

After they had been driving for three hours Stirling called another halt, and Sadler was summoned to the front of the convoy for another confab. Telling his commander he was confident they were still on the correct bearing, Sadler estimated they had ten miles until the target. It was at this point, recalled Carol Mather, that Stirling told the raiders to make a final check of their weapons and ammunition. He also issued a final set of instructions, a reminder of the plan of attack:

> At the edge of the aerodrome form line abreast and all guns spray the area – when I advance follow me in your two columns and on my green Very light open fire outwards at the aircraft. Follow exactly in each other's tracks 5 yards apart, speed not more than 4 mph – return to the rendezvous independently moving only by night.

The men mounted their vehicles and the column moved on towards Sidi Haneish.

The next hour's driving was interrupted twice by swift tyre changes. (Sadler recalled that the jeeps' Mohawk tyres were prone to punctures and it was with much relief when they were subsequently replaced with another brand.) Suddenly the men sensed they had emerged from the vast isolation of the desert into a region recently occupied by men and their vehicles. 'The change was scarcely perceptible but most of us had been in the desert long enough to know,' reflected Stephen Hastings. The terrain felt different, reacted differently to the wheels, as they passed over old track marks. Then they received gruesome confirmation that they were indeed no longer passing over pristine desert. 'We descended across an old battlefield, where some of our corpses were lying still unburied in the full moonlight,' wrote Mather. 'The burnt out tanks and corpses looked cold and comfortless and I took countless swigs of rum.'

As the men looked uneasily around their attention was brought back

THE FLYING DESERT FOX

Following the suicide of Rommel in October 1944, ordered by Hitler because of his belief that his Field Marshal had in some way been involved in the failed attempt to assassinate him the previous July, his family gathered the papers he had left behind. Collated, they subsequently formed 'The Rommel Papers', throwing a fascinating light on the man and his methods. With the aid of Rommel's wife, and his son, Manfred, renowned British military historian Basil Liddell-Hart published the *Papers* to worldwide acclaim in 1953. Reflecting on the desert war in 1942, Rommel had this to say about the importance of achieving aerial supremacy in North Africa:

'A second essential condition for an army to be able to stand in battle is parity or at least something approaching parity in the air. If the enemy has air supremacy and makes full use of it, then one's own command is forced to suffer the following limitations and disadvantages:
'By using his strategic air force, the enemy can strangle one's supplies, especially if they have to be carried across the sea.
'The enemy can wage the battle of attrition from the air.
'Intensive exploration by the enemy of his air superiority gives rise to far-reaching tactical limitations for one's own command.
'In future the battle on the ground will be preceded by the battle in the air. This will determine which of the contestants has to suffer the operational and tactical disadvantages detailed above ... in our case, neither of the conditions I have described were in the slightest degree fulfilled and we had to suffer the consequences.'

On the night of 26 July 1942 the desert war was still very much in the balance. Just eight days earlier Rommel had written to his wife, telling her, 'Yesterday was a particularly hard and critical day. We pulled through again. But it can't go on like it for long, otherwise the front will crack. Militarily, this is the most difficult period I've ever been through.'

Supplies and lines of communication were perilously stretched for Rommel across the Libyan Desert. What he did not want was the destruction of numerous aircraft to further hamper his capabilities.

Erwin Rommel (back to camera), aka the Desert Fox, had the respect of the SAS.

to the front of the column by a German Very light away on the horizon – nothing to do with them. All the same, the raiders' hearts began to beat a little faster: they were nearing the target. A few minutes later the convoy stopped and once more Sadler jogged to its head as his commander searched for signs of the target. 'David [Stirling] sent for me and said politely, "Where the hell is it? Have we gone wrong?"' recalled Sadler. 'I said, "No, I reckon, it's two miles ahead". And as I said it the lights came on right across the airstrip. I thought, "Ah, this is my great moment of triumph". I got a tremendous kick out of it.'

Although this photograph was not taken before the Sidi Haneish raid, it nonetheless depicts the sight that must have greeted the Axis forces when the attack began.

For a terrible moment the men thought their presence had been detected but then 'we heard an aircraft overhead, it was circling low'. Mather looked up with the rest of the men and realised why the landing strip had been illuminated.

Stirling ordered his men back into their jeeps and the raiders set off for the aerodrome, manoeuvring into the formation they had rehearsed. Carol Mather pulled out to the edge of the right flank, Stephen Hastings to the edge of the left, both officers working furiously to keep in line 'over uneven ground with vision limited to 15 dusty yards'. Overhead the sound of the incoming aircraft's engines grew louder and suddenly a green and a red light burst in the sky as the pilot fired the recognition signal.

A couple of minutes later the aircraft began its descent into Sidi Haneish, so Stirling picked up the pace of their advance from their initial 4mph. 'Drivers strained to keep formation,' said Hastings. 'My jeep crashed into a trench of some kind. I changed gear and the little vehicle just pulled up the other side.'

Jim Almonds, also in the left-hand column, drove into the same trench, in fact a concealed anti-tank ditch skirting the airfield perimeter. Almonds and his gunners were catapulted from the jeep but none was hurt in the crash. The jeep, however, was stuck and no amount of heaving would shift it from the trench. Almonds ran after Stirling, who had halted in readiness for the assault, and informed his commander of what had occurred. 'Bad luck,' said Stirling. 'You'd better join Sadler.'

As his two gunners were dispersed into other vehicles, Almonds jumped into Sadler's jeep as the navigator left the convoy and headed for the south-east corner of the airfield. As well as being detailed to collect any stragglers, Sadler had been given a second task by Stirling. 'David had asked, or rather told me, to take photographs of the raid,' explained Sadler. 'So I had in the jeep my camera and a roll of film.'

One account of the raid, described in Virginia Cowles's *The Phantom Major*, says that Stirling chased the descending aircraft on to Sidi Haneish; in reality the plane had already landed by the time the raiders had reached the airfield. According to Stephen Hastings's account, a solitary rifle shot from a bewildered sentry signalled the start of the raid.

The opening burst

'We formed up line abreast, halted and suddenly fired our 60 [*sic*.] guns, a minute's fire to spray the defences,' recalled Mather. Hastings looked on as his jeep shook with the fire poured on to the airfield by his two gunners: 'First, one tentative burst, then the full ear-splitting cacophony roaring and spitting. Streams of red and white colour shot through the darkness, struck the ground and cascaded upwards in a thousand crazy arcs, criss-crossing each other.'

Hastings saw a myriad of little white flames erupting over the field as incendiary bullets hit the ground and caught fire. He glimpsed the eerie silhouettes of terrified men running for cover, their senses scrambled by the bedlam breaking around them.

One defender managed to collect his thoughts long enough to switch off the airfield's landing lights, while the pilot inside the recently arrived aircraft – still going through his post-flight procedures – turned off his engine and lights. Simultaneously, the 16 jeeps ceased firing, and for a few surreal moments peace reigned in the desert. Not for long. 'David's green Very light signal broke in the centre,' remembered Hastings, who was at the back of the convoy in the left-hand column opposite Mather's vehicle at the rear of the right. The terrain was no longer uneven but was flat and solid and for a brief while Stirling increased the pace as they neared the dispersal area. Hastings had the whiff of cordite in his nostrils and around his feet a carpet of empty cartridge cases as he crouched over the wheel waiting for the next outbreak of firing.

It began, he estimated, two or three minutes after Stirling's Very light as

Paddy Mayne in action (overleaf)

Once the SAS raiders has cruised slowly down the runway, laying waste to any enemy aircraft that came within range of their awesome firepower, David Stirling called a halt. Standing up in his jeep, the SAS commander sounded a horn, the signal for the column to wheel and skirt around the airfield, seeking out fresh targets among the Messerschmitts, Junkers, Stukas and Heinkels. Suddenly a figure leapt from one of the SAS vehicles and bounded across the landing strip with something clutched in his hand. It was the unmistakable shape of Paddy Mayne. Reaching up to one of the few untouched aircraft, the big Irishman planted a Lewes bomb high up on the wing near the engine. As the column began to swing round one of the SAS officers, Lt Stephen Hastings, recalled that as his vehicle passed the aircraft 'there was a tremendous explosion which momentarily stunned us. One wing sagged to the ground and the big aircraft caught fire'.

their commander slowed to a crawl. Capt Jellicoe wrote in his operational report that by the time they were on the landing strip itself, speed had been 'reduced to one or two miles an hour'.

Jimmy Storie was in the jeep driven by David Russell and remembered: 'We were driving at about 2, 2 ½ miles an hour, quite slowly. Just me and David in the jeep, and we didn't communicate about the right speed to go at, you just kept your distance … gun discipline was vital. We had to keep in a strict formation two abreast, firing outwards the whole time.' According to Johnny Cooper, 'It was like a duck shoot, pouring Vickers fire into the planes and seeing them explode.'

By the time the rear jeeps – those of Hastings and Mather – were on the landing strip the heat was so intense it singed hair and eyebrows. Hastings saw two figures cowering beneath the fuselage of a burning twin-engine Junkers 52 transport aircraft. His rear gunner – regrettably, Hastings neglected to record the names of his gunners – also spotted them, yelling over the din:

'There's two Jerries!'

'Well, shoot at them; go on shoot at them.'

The rear gunner fired a burst in the direction of the men and Hastings, unable to see through the smoke, shouted:

A smiling Paddy Mayne. He was Stirling's second-in-command and the most lethal British commando of the war.

'Did you get them?'

'I don't know, sir.'

Opposite Hastings's vehicle Carol Mather shot a sideways glance at the aircraft as Cpls Bob Lilley and David Lambie pumped bullets into the 'Messerschmitts, Junkers, Stukas and Heinkels that lay all around us'. He recalled: 'Clouds obscured the moon, and one after another the planes burst with flames … some of the aircraft would only be 15 yards away, and as I passed them at the end of the column, they would glow red and exploded with a deafening "phut" and there would be great heat.'

Stirling then sounded a horn – some reports have said it was a whistle, but Jellicoe's operational report, written a few weeks after the event was adamant it was a horn – the signal for the column to wheel and skirt around the airfield, seeking out fresh targets. For a moment or two the raiders halted as they prepared for the move. During the pause Hastings spotted the unmistakable figure of Paddy Mayne leap from his jeep and sprint towards an untouched aircraft where he planted a Lewes bomb high up on the wing near the engine. The column began to swing and just as Hastings's vehicle passed the aircraft 'there was a tremendous explosion which momentarily stunned us. One wing sagged to the ground and the big aircraft caught fire'.

Mather recalled: 'we were swinging round for a second visit when an AA [anti-aircraft] gun 300 yards away opened up on us wildly'. Hastings said that as well as an AA gun, there was also incoming mortar fire, small arms fire and the heavy thump of two Italian Breda cannons. 'Ponka-ponka-ponk – the big 20mm red tracer bullets flashing over the heads of the jeep crew,' he recalled.

Still the SAS gunners continued to pour a withering fire into everything they could see, which by now included two or three large tents as they moved away from the dispersal area towards the outskirts of the airfield. 'We got a load of fire from the guards,' said Storie. 'We knew we were under fire … but with our guns firing the only way we knew was when rounds whistled over our heads or in among you.'

The fire was getting a little too close for comfort for Hastings, who screamed at his gunners to silence the enemy. Four Vickers pumped out bullets, but then,

> a few seconds later we were rewarded by a long burst from the Breda. Big red streamers shot past and sailed away into the night. Then they hit us. I felt something hot pass most uncomfortably close beneath my seat. Clang! My face and my gunners were doused in oil. There was a moment of blindness. I wiped the oil out of my eyes, the jeep swerved violently, hit a bump, recovered itself and miraculously continued.

Not as fortunate as Hastings was Stirling's own vehicle. 'We got a shell through the cylinder head and had to abandon our jeep,' said Johnny Cooper. 'Sandy Scratchley's [jeep] pulled up alongside and we hopped on board. Sandy's rear gunner was lying dead in the back.' Twenty-one year-old LBdr John Robson, a Royal Artilleryman from County Durham, had been killed instantly by cannon fire to the head.

Regrouping on the airfield

Invisible in the dark periphery of the airfield, Stirling waited until all the jeeps had assembled, then he yelled 'Switch off'.

'Anybody hurt?' enquired Stirling, who was pleased to learn Robson was the sole casualty. 'Any ammunition left?'

Back came a variety of responses: 'only one drum', 'two drums', 'half a drum'.

'All right, we'll have one more go over this side of the dispersal area then beat it,' said Stirling. 'Don't fire unless you're certain of getting a target and watch out for those bloody Breda guns.'

The jeeps moved off and for a couple of hundred yards came across nothing to wreck. Then a Messerschmitt Bf 109 loomed out of the darkness and a dozen guns ripped open its fuselage before the machine exploded in a fireball. They drove on searching for aircraft, tents, guards, anything, but saw only some ruined stone outbuildings, which nonetheless were hosed in

0230HRS,
JULY 27

The watching LRDG
patrol leaves the
burning airfield

bullets, sending 'coloured ricochets darting in all directions'. Then, recalled Hastings, 'the line turned gradually left-handed, the pace increased and our flight began'.

The raiders' escape

David Russell and Jimmy Storie encountered a problem as they made good their escape from the scene of the crime. 'He ran into some bloody barbed wire and it was all round the wheels so I had to nip out with a big pair of pliers to snip it away,' remembered Storie. 'David was moaning, and anyway we got all this cut and … we caught up with the rest of the jeeps.'

Russell joined the officers gathered around Stirling and listened as he told them they would 'split up now into various parties and make for the rendezvous independently of each other. The idea was to get as far away as we could in two and a half hours, and to "camouflage down" before the daylight should betray our whereabouts to an angry and determined enemy in the air'.

Stirling told his officers that it was up to them what course they took to reach the rendezvous, but that everyone should try and cross to the 'west of the big track with the telegraph poles running along it, which led from Bagush to Qara at the north-western tip of the Depression'. This track, warned Stirling, would likely be the first place the enemy would search in their hunt for the raiders who had just visited destruction on Sidi Haneish.

According to Hastings, six jeeps had been hit during the raid but only three had been put out of action, including Almonds's at the very start. The raiders began to split up: the three French vehicles moved off, then Stirling's party comprising four jeeps, then Mayne's of a similar number. Mather led three jeeps away from Sidi Haneish having glanced back in wonderment at what they had done. 'We had burnt 30 aircraft, damaged more and lost … one man killed. The whole thing had taken 15 minutes.'

Two of the jeeps in Mather's small convoy that comprised eight men had 'irreparable' punctures, but there was nothing to do but drive on and hope for the best. 'There was about an hour and a half's darkness left, then the sun would rise and we must seek cover for the day,' he reflected. 'We drove very fast watching the stars for our direction and watching for that paleness to appear, which meant dawn.'

Sadler and Almonds

Mike Sadler had passed the time during the raid taking timed exposures of the burning planes and admiring, with Jim Almonds, the handiwork of his comrades. 'The whole thing was very impressive and I had a ringside view of the tracer fire and the aircraft going up,' he reflected. 'But also impressive was the speed at which the Germans got the airfield working again, within an hour of the attack they had other aircraft coming in.'

Sadler, who was not surprised by the success of the raid, had instructions to remain at the south-east corner of the airfield for an hour after the raid before making for the rendezvous. 'I didn't get away from there until just before dawn and luckily there was a sea mist as we left.'

As Sadler drove through the mist he saw vague shapes up ahead on the road. 'It was a German column that had been sent out to look for us,' he said, adding that it was a 'rather a nasty surprise' as they drew level with the rear of the column that had stopped momentarily.

Bearded, unkempt, coated in dust from the previous night's long drive across the desert, Sadler, and Almonds knew they had to try and bluff their way to safety. 'We went on driving past the column but with increasing speed. It was just a case of holding your nerve and hoping the Germans didn't twig it but thought we were part of the same organization. It was a nerve-racking moment.'

Sadler's luck held and within a few minutes he had left the column far behind, heading south towards the rendezvous. Already well away from Sidi Haneish by the time dawn arrived on the 27th was Capt Nick Wilder and his patrol of the LRDG. Since waving goodbye to the SAS nearly 12 hours earlier, Wilder had had plenty of adventure, as he noted in the patrol diary:

At latitude 31° 01'north, longitude 37° 19' E, T Patrol struck minefield. T.3 [each vehicle in an LRDG patrol had a number] truck had to be abandoned after hitting a mine. After finding a track through the mines, four Germans were found asleep on the road-side. Impossible to take them with the patrol, so dropped them in the desert some three miles east of the road. Finally reached L.Gs but by this time were about one hour late and the paratroops had started operations.

Graham Rose and Jimmy Storie were original members of the SAS and are seen here behind the lines in the summer of 1942.

Kufra Oasis, although larger than Siwa, was even more remote. It proved a valuable base for the LRDG and SAS during the desert war.

Wilder counted 15 burning aircraft before deciding to withdraw from Sidi Haneish at 0230 hours on 27 July. A little over five hours later the LRDG patrol was spotted near Qaret Hireimas by two reconnaissance aircraft and the pilots radioed their position to a 'German–Italian column of some 30 vehicles'. Wilder described what happened next in the diary:

> T.5 and T.6 were both engaged by a 40mm machine gun from the east, at a range of 600 yards with four more trucks coming around from the north. There was no sign of T.4 or T1 who were on the other side of the hill in another wadi. The opposition being too hot, we withdrew to the mouth of the depression to avoid being cut off. We were followed by two trucks for approximately three miles. On reaching the depression at 1600 hours, we camped for the day, and waited for T1 and T4. At 1800 hours there was no sign of the remainder of the patrol. OC [officer commanding] Party decided to return as two thirds of the patrol, and only two trucks, were not of much use. Also, rations and water were short, our supplies being left at the base before operations on the LGs began the previous night.

With at least six enemy vehicles still in hot pursuit, four of which were trucks containing soldiers, Wilder drove through the night and the next day towards Mena until, later on 28 July, they ran into a Guards Patrol of the LRDG who escorted them back to their base at Kufra, having informed Wilder that the missing two trucks had made it back safely to the SAS hideout at Bir el Quseir.

Wilder had been under the impression that the two trucks, T4 and T1, had been destroyed in the initial contact with the 30-strong Axis patrol.

When reunited at Kufra a few days later he learned that the smoke he saw billowing up on the other side of the hill from where he was came from one of the reconnaissance aircraft. The pilot of one Fiesler Storch, seeing the two LRDG trucks, had assumed they were German and descended. Merlyn Craw opened fire at the aircraft the moment its engine was off and out tumbled two very surprised Germans, one of whom was a doctor.

Mather's party

Carol Mather's party of three jeeps had driven hard over the desert as, above them, the night sky began slowly to lighten. It was Mather's aim to cross the telegraph track – which Stirling had warned would be their pursuer's first marker point – before dawn. Fortunately the sea mist that had enveloped Sadler and Almonds also aided their flight from Sidi Haneish. Then, just as the early morning sun burnt off the last of its protective blanket, there only a few hundred yards away was the telegraph track. 'We became fearful of aircraft but took the risk and tore down the track on our tyreless rims bumping and rattling over the rocky surface until we came to those stones placed in a triangle, which had been put there the night before to serve as a guide for our return,' recalled Mather.

Now the small convoy turned west on a bearing of 320 degrees and hit the accelerator, determined to put a couple of miles between them and the track before finding a place to lie up for the rest of the day. A low escarpment ran parallel to the route the three jeeps were on and, for a moment, Mather was tempted to hide the jeeps in its shadow. But that could become a death trap if spotted by aircraft, so he drove on a short while until they saw some thick camel thorn a foot high. Dispersing the jeeps among the bushes, the eight men then camouflaged the vehicles as best they could. Mather recalled the event:

> We felt very bare and exposed in this spot but decided to revive our spirits with a little breakfast. No sooner had the tea come up to a boil and the sausages started sizzling than the first aircraft appeared. 'Aircraft!' someone said in that quiet and urgent voice which we'd learned to dread, and we all froze while it passed harmlessly over – a Stuka weaving and searching its way down the long low escarpment. I told the men to scatter themselves

Escaping and evading (overleaf)

Early on the morning of July 27 Lt Carol Mather and his patrol stopped for breakfast having driven through the night across the desert. Deciding to conceal their jeeps among some foot-high camel thorn, Mather and his men began brewing some tea and cooking some sausages. Suddenly one of the eight SAS soldiers gave a cry: 'Aircraft!' The men froze as the lone Stuka passed harmlessly overhead and on to the nearby long low escarpment where it began looking for the raiders. Mather ordered his men to move 400 yards away from the vehicles and lie down among the camel thorn in case more aircraft should appear. They did. 'Soon the sky became alive with aircraft, circling angrily round and round, like a swarm of angry bees, out to seek vengeance on the destruction of the night before,' recalled Mather. For 12 hours he and his men lay among the camel thorn under a broiling sun as the Axis aircraft searched out the raiders. Despite the best efforts of the Luftwaffe none of their pilots spotted the camouflaged vehicles or the men who had caused such damage a few hours earlier on Sidi Haneish.

It was not the Axis fighter aircraft that the SAS and LRDG feared most in the desert, it was the slower reconnaissance machines that were better at spotting the raiders from above.

400 yards away from the vehicles and not to move, put a few finishing touches to the camouflage, sorrowfully left the breakfast and then walked slowly away myself looking over my shoulder for aeroplanes and stopping and listening every few paces.

Mather lay down among the camel thorn and did what the rest of his men were doing – waited and prayed and disciplined himself not to move a muscle in the searing heat. 'Soon the sky became alive with aircraft, circling angrily round and round, like a swarm of angry bees, out to seek vengeance on the destruction of the night before,' he remembered.

For 12 hours Mather and his men lay among the camel thorn as the Axis aircraft searched out the raiders who they knew to be somewhere beneath them. Eventually the sun began to lose its vigour before dipping below the horizon in the direction the raiders must follow. The ordeal had tested them all, particularly one young soldier who had been slightly wounded in the raid. Cpl Bob Lilley, 'rather a motherly person', according to Mather, tended the man, 'along with the rest of us with a fatalistic expression on his face, ready to be our guide, philosopher or friend if the need arose'

With the night having reclaimed the desert, Mather's party threw off the camouflage nets and filled up their vehicles with petrol from the jerricans. Then Mather walked a short distance away from the jeeps and took a bearing of 320 degrees on his magnetic compass, at the same time locating a corresponding constellation of stars as an additional navigational aid.

They drove through the rest of the evening of 27 July but at 0300 hours on the 28th Mather realised they were lost, having covered what he calculated to be 13 miles. 'To concentrate on driving and watching the stars was enough, there was no room for hopes or fears,' he said. There was only one course of action to take, to drive on for a few miles and then lie up and wait for the dawn. 'Tomorrow could take care of itself,' Mather told himself, as they bumped over the desert for a further five miles before pulling up in a small depression. 'Suddenly light of heart we unstrapped our bedding, laid it out on the sand and went to sleep,' remembered Mather.

He dozed for an hour and on waking told Cpls Lambie and Lilley he was going for a reconnoitre. Lambie went too, while Lilley stayed with the wounded man. Dawn was just breaking as the pair drove straight towards the moon, which was on the exact line of their bearing. 'It was low in the sky and turning pink,' recorded Mather, 'and I was just saying to Lambie how fortunate it was that now the stars had gone in, that we had the moon to drive on – when suddenly through the mist we saw a drop, and there was a cairn.'

Mather braked and stared at the cairn, fighting the feeling of excitement taking hold of his body. He looked at Lambie and, with a poker face, said that he thought the cairn looked familiar; was it the same one that he and Stephen Hastings had walked to every day as they waited for Stirling to return from Cairo a week or so earlier? 'Are you sure?' asked Lambie. Mather, still playing it cool, replied that he thought he was right. And that if he was there should also be a small wadi nearby which could be used as a bay for lorries.

Mather started. There in the direction he was pointing he could just make out a three tonner draped with a camouflage net. He wanted to shout for joy, but he knew if he did Lambie would see that his officer had been harbouring doubts about their exact location. Mather recalled:

I told Lambie casually that I thought we were about right and didn't show any excitement, and a great smile spread over his face. We drove the half mile back to the others, shouted 'wake up, we're home, come on, pack up and get the engines started'. Then we dropped down the cliff, over the familiar bumps and along the cliff edge stirring up great clouds of talcum powder dust until we reached the long cave. Then up and into it with the three jeeps making thunder in its caves and waking the sleepers on the ground.

One of the sleepers woken from his slumber by the cacophonous return of Carol Mather's jeep party was Malcolm Pleydell, the SAS officer. After waving off the raiding party 36 hours earlier, he and the rest of the men detailed to remain at the hideout had idled away the time, eating their meals cold – in case roving aircraft should spot the smoke – reading and speculating on the success or otherwise of the raid.

Mather's three jeeps were the first ones home, and the rest of the morning – once Pleydell had seen to the wounded man – was spent listening to accounts of the raid. Then, around 1600 hours, the sentry alerted his comrades to the approach of four more vehicles. Pleydell rushed up to the lookout point on the escarpment's pimple and immediately recognised the figure in the lead jeep, 'as massive and unconcerned as ever, hunched up and dwarfing both driver and vehicle'.

Once Paddy Mayne reached the sanctuary of the escarpment, he climbed out of the vehicle and found a quiet spot to lie down and read. Pleydell strolled over to ask how things had gone.

The bones of a camel were a grim reminder to the SAS of how cruel the desert could be.

'Och, it was quite a good craic,' replied the Irishman.

'How many planes did you get?'

'It's hard to say. Forty maybe. I doubt that we'll be claiming more than thirty.' The official tally credited to the raid was 18 aircraft destroyed and a further 12 damaged.

Mayne told Pleydell about the death of John Robson and the final question of the conversation was asked by the doctor. He wanted to know why Mayne came in during the day?

'I got bored waiting,' replied Mayne. 'And there were no planes about.'

A few minutes after Pleydell had left Mayne alone with his book there was another cry from the sentry. Aircraft!

Pleydell ducked into one of the caves and then cautiously peeped out from behind the tarpaulin: 'Six Junkers 87s were flying straight down the wadi, about one thousand feet up,' he remarked. 'In front of, and behind them were two M.E. 109s, weaving and zigzagging across the line of their path. They looked dark and aggressive, and full of foreboding.'

None of the airmen inside the eight German aircraft saw anything suspicious about the escarpment and the flight flew on to continue its search. Pleydell, meanwhile, wondered what could have happened to the rest of the raiders.

Stirling's party

On leaving Sidi Haneish, Stirling's party of four jeeps and 14 men – comprising those of George Jellicoe, Sandy Scratchley and Stephen Hastings – had driven south-west through dense patches of camel thorn that reached

MORNING, JULY 28

Mather's three jeeps return to rendezvous

as high as the running boards of the four vehicles as they passed. The convoy roared up an escarpment and changed bearing, 'heading well west of south', as the dawn began to break. Suddenly Hastings's jeep spluttered and died, its engine unable to bear the rigours being asked of it. The column stopped and while the men transferred to other jeeps, Hastings set a ten-minute fuse on a Lewes bomb and left it in his vehicle.

In vain they searched for the telegraph track, their relief at the early morning mist that reduced visibility to 20yd tempered by the knowledge it would not last long once the sun got to work. They were still in the open when the fog vanished, but the desert came to their aid once more. 'We found ourselves on the edge of a small escarpment dropping about 15 feet,' recalled Hastings. 'Below was a large bowl-shaped depression a quarter of a

AFTERNOON, JULY 28

Mayne's four jeeps also return to the rendezvous

A desert conference between SAS and LRDG officers. The two special forces shared a great mutual respect that was used to deadly effect against Axis targets.

mile broad, its walls cut by fairly deep wadis with thick scrub up to 3 or 4 feet high.' It was perfect and within minutes the three jeeps and 14 men had disappeared from sight.

The first thing they did once safely concealed was to brew up, using two old tins, the bottom one containing sand and shrub doused in petrol and set alight, the top one full of water. After they'd drunk their tea, LBdr John Robson was laid to rest in a hole dug by two of his comrades. Once the body had been lowered into the grave, the men gently covered the corpse with sand and then placed a couple of large rocks on top. A cross fashioned out of a ration box was stuck at the head of the grave and then the men bowed their heads for a few moments, each alone with his thoughts. Robson had come up from Cairo with Stirling a few days before; no one really knew him, except for the 'cheery red face and a shock of black hair'. Nonetheless, thought Hastings, somebody must love him, thousands of miles away in England, blissfully unaware he was now being laid to rest in the middle of the Libyan Desert. Hastings 'looked around at the loneliness, the vague shapeless loneliness stretching for so many hundreds of forgotten miles' and realized that 'probably no living thing would ever pass this grave again except perhaps the gazelle'.

The burial over, Stirling ordered his men under cover and reminded them to keep both water consumption and movement to a minimum for the next dozen hours or so. A few minutes later they heard the sound of aircraft, but they passed by on their way east and throughout the rest of the day the only interruption to their solitude was the occasional plane.

They emerged from their bowl-shaped depression at sundown on 27 July and resumed their search for the telegraph track. After nearly two hours they found it; that was the good news. The bad news was a serious puncture to one of the three jeeps that proved irreparable, because they had run out of spare tyres. Reluctantly, Stirling decided that they would have to continue in the vehicle even though it meant reducing their pace to that of the 'lame duck' jeep.

On they went, the men all shivering inside their overcoats as they balanced precariously in the back of the jeeps. After another two hours Stirling stopped and he and Johnny Cooper consulted the map. Cooper was sure he knew where they were, approximately 36 miles from the rendezvous. A short while later the third jeep suffered another blown tyre and Stirling reached the end of his patience, ordering its driver to keep going on the bearing while the other two vehicles pressed on. He reassured the driver and the other occupants they would be back to collect them once they had reached the rendezvous.

As dawn approached on the morning of 28 July Stirling and his reduced party remained in the open searching for familiar signs. They found none. No doubt about it, they were lost. Then from some way behind them they heard what Hastings described as a strange noise, a 'clankety-clank, bang, clankety-clank, bang'. From over the ridge to their right hove slowly into view the third jeep. 'With one last scrunch and clank it came to a halt,' recalled Hastings. 'The driver folded his arms and leant on the wheel, while the crew stared gloomily down at us.' For a moment or two no one said anything, then everyone dissolved into laughter.

By dusk on the 28th they still had not found the rendezvous, but nor had they been found by enemy aircraft. There was no point searching by night, not if they couldn't find their way by day, so they slept soundly, waking at first light on the 29th. Spirits were low, said Hastings, with everyone believing they were well and truly lost in the desert, and with only enough petrol for 5 more miles.

Their progress was slow, the third jeep still making its comical noise, and soon the column came to a halt. Johnny Cooper jumped down from the lead jeep and trudged slowly forward to the lip of the same escarpment that Mather had stood on a day earlier. Hastings saw Cooper suddenly whirl round and come running back, waving his arms excitedly. They had reached the rendezvous and below the escarpment were a truck and a group of their comrades enjoying breakfast.

When Stirling's party reached the main base at Bir el Quseir their joy was short-lived. The French jeeps had arrived a few hours earlier, having buried André Zirnheld. Capt Augustin Jordan explained that when the mist had cleared on the morning of 27 July they had sheltered in the crevice of a small cliff close to the telegraph track. But a flight of three Stukas had found them in the early afternoon and in the nine attacks that followed, Zirnheld was mortally wounded. He died a short while later and was buried in a small wadi, his comrades writing on a cross made out of a packing case:

'André Zirnheld, Mort pour la France, 27 Juillet, 1942'

Mike Sadler and Jim Almonds had enjoyed greater fortune than the French. Having driven past the German column shortly after dawn on 27 July, the pair had had another lucky escape a short while later. Deciding to lie up in a clump of bushes between two knolls, Sadler went off on foot for a reconnoitre. 'I hadn't gone far when I saw that Jim Almonds was waving at me,' he recalls. Sadler made his way back to the camouflaged jeep and was told in a whisper by Almonds that 'just over the other side of the hill was a German recovery team, recovering vehicles from some battle'. The pair spent the rest of the day under cover while the Germans worked, eventually emerging at night to continue their way home.

Debrief

The raiders had breakfast on 29 July, once they were all safely back at the hideout, and the two German prisoners captured by Merlyn Craw were introduced. The pilot of the Storch was one of Rommel's small team of pilots while the doctor was Baron von Lutterotti, who unintentionally provided the comic turn for the day in talking about his pre-war holiday in the Essex town of Clacton-on-Sea. According to Carol Mather:

All he would say was 'I went up for pleasure but it ended unhappily', And then they talked about 'Clicton-on-Sea', which he said he had visited. And so we all roared with laughter and went about repeating amongst ourselves, 'I went up for pleasure but it ended unhappily'. But we laughed even louder when George [Jellicoe] discovered that he had stayed at the doctor's house in Berlin before the war. It was all too much, thirty aeroplanes destroyed, all of us back except two, the exhilaration of a morning in the desert after a night of anxiety, no sleep for 48 hours and now – these Germans, it was too much.

'THE PARATROOPERS' PRAYER'

Born in Paris in March 1913, André Zirnheld's family came from Alsace in eastern France, an area long fought over by France and Germany. Zirnheld was a fierce French patriot and he was distraught when he learned of his country's surrender in June 1940 – he was teaching philosophy in Syria at the time. Zirnheld crossed into British-held Palestine and by the end of 1941 had obtained his commission in the Free French Army. He volunteered to serve in the French paratroop section that was assigned to the SAS and did so with distinction until his death at Sidi Haneish. Among his personal effects left at Kabrit was the following poem, written by Zirnheld in April 1938, and entitled 'The Prayer'. Subsequently adopted by France's postwar paratroopers, the verse is now known as 'The Paratrooper's Prayer' and is recited by airborne troops throughout the world.

> I'm asking You God, to give me what You have left.
> Give me those things which others never ask of You.
> I don't ask You for rest, or tranquility.
> Not that of the spirit, the body, or the mind.
> I don't ask You for wealth, or success, or even health.
> All those things are asked of You so much Lord,
> that you can't have any left to give.
> Give me instead Lord what You have left.
> Give me what others don't want.
> I want uncertainty and doubt.
> I want torment and battle.
> And I ask that You give them to me now and forever Lord,
> so I can be sure to always have them,
> because I won't always have the strength to ask again.
> But give me also the courage, the energy,
> and the spirit to face them.
> I ask You these things Lord,
> because I can't ask them of myself.

It turned out that the Jellicoe family was acquainted with the von Lutterottis, though George – to much guffawing from his comrades – denied ever having stayed with the Baron. He may have had lunch with him, he admitted, but that was all.

After breakfast Stirling assembled the men for a debrief. The soldiers gathered in the shade around their commander expecting warm words of congratulations, but their smugness was soon disabused.

It's pretty plain that you think you have done jolly well. But if you want to know what I think – I'll tell you. It wasn't good enough! It wasn't nearly good enough! Some of you were out of position, some of you were firing at planes you could only just see, and a lot of you were firing wildly. You must shoot low rather than high. I told you that before we started. And you must save your ammunition for the targets you can hit for certain. Other people will be shooting up those which are outside your range. (Carol Mather papers, IWM)

Stirling continued in a similar vein for several minutes, admonishing his men for their profligacy. One or two soldiers grumbled that they would have destroyed more aircraft if they had gone in on foot – like they used to. Stirling gave such dissenters short shrift. 'You couldn't!' he exclaimed. 'Get that quite clear in your minds. There were far too many sentry posts and ground defences about. You would never have got anywhere' (Carol Mather papers, IWM).

These stones in the desert designate a praying place for nomadic travellers.

After dismissal, most of the men drifted away to find a quiet corner in which to sleep, but one or two stayed behind to discuss points with Stirling who, in an avuncular manner, offered more words of constructive criticism. All in all, opined Pleydell, it had been a brilliantly judged debrief by Stirling, 'for it stopped the men from becoming too complacent or thinking this sort of work was all plain sailing'.

Stirling had also spoken to his officers and agreed that at sundown they would move to a new base, approximately 15 miles west of their present location. Until then they were to rest. Stirling and Mayne, however, sat down and began planning fresh raids on the enemy beginning with one that very night.

The overriding issue was one of resupply, but during his stay in Cairo earlier in the month Stirling had considered the challenge of keeping the SAS supplied hundreds of miles deep in the desert. AVM Bruce Bennett of the Joint Planning Staff had initially proposed dropping fresh supplies of food and equipment by parachute, but he and Stirling then decided the best solution would be to send in a Bombay bomber to an emergency landing strip not too far away.

However, before Stirling could summon up MEHQ on the wireless set, they received a signal from Cairo instructing him and his men to return to Egypt for a new operation. Stirling was livid and signalled back the fact, but it did him no good. MEHQ replied that the proposed 'operation was of vital importance' but that, rest assured, he would have his 'usual free hand' in planning the role of the SAS.

The signal then detailed how Stirling and his men would make their return to Cairo – on board one of the Bombays of 216 Squadron. Furious, Stirling could do nothing but acquiesce to his superiors, though he still dispatched a raiding party that evening to attack enemy transport in the built-up region behind the El Alamein area. Chris Bailey, David Russell, Augustin Jordan and Carol Mather set off and met with varying degrees of success over the 48 hours that ensued. Russell, using his flawless German with a Bavarian accent, tricked several lone enemy vehicles into stopping by pretending his jeep had broken down. The moment the enemy fell for the ruse their fate was sealed. Mather, meanwhile, had a stroke of good fortune when his jeep saw a column of German panzers approaching. 'We counted the tanks as they passed and were just beginning to heave a sigh of relief when there was a grinding and clanking above the cave where Lambie and I crouched,' recalled Mather. 'A tank crossed immediately over our heads. Great chunks of rock came cascading down, and at one moment we thought the roof was going to collapse. It was almost impossible for them to miss us from above, but they did, and continued on their way.'

When Mather and the other three patrols returned to the escarpment they discovered the bulk of their comrades had been flown back to Cairo in a Bombay. Sandy Scratchley and Stephen Hasting were among the 30-strong rearguard left behind by Stirling to wait for the patrols.

They were obliged to return by jeep and truck (25 in total) by the shortest route possible to avoid the enemy, and that entailed crossing the treacherous and mysterious Qattara Depression, a journey that Mather described a year later in an article written for the *Royal Geographical Journal*. The Depression, shaped like a teardrop and covering an area twice as large as the Lebanon, was a fascination for European scientists and explorers, all of whom devoured Mather's account of its crossing. At times, as they drove down a track towards the bottom of the Depression, there was a 'park-like appearance' to their surroundings, but once at the bottom the terrain changed as they surveyed the Depression from under a 400ft cliff. 'We could see as far as the eye stretched – to the east a firm but broken coast, to the south-east a flat gravel plain [but] we were unable to see any sign of bog or marsh.'

As they drove east the ground became rockier for a spell and then they finally hit the infamous hard salt crust that had earned the Depression its impassable reputation. One of the jeeps slowly disappeared in a bog, so the other three halted, the drivers terrified of their vehicles suffering a similar fate. Three jeeps fanned out looking for a place to ford the bog and finally one was found, a 10ft wide dyke of soft sand that could be bridged using

sand channels and tarpaulins. 'It had to be done very quickly because the stationary vehicles on the near side soon began sinking slowly through the [salt] crust,' wrote Mather. 'In fact we were too late with our last three-tonner for when its turn came to take the jump it had sunk up to its axles and soon the tailboard began to disappear.'

Finally all the remaining vehicles were across and to the soldiers' relief the surface became firmer, eventually opening on to a flat gravel plain. 'We halted for a few moments to get our direction,' said Mather. 'Took a bearing on a low constellation of stars, switched on all our headlights and raced at 50 mph towards the north-east. The dawn was just beginning to break, the billiard table surface lasted, and we covered thirty miles in less than an hour.'

When they finally reached Cairo, Hastings and Mather made for the Mena House Hotel, below the majestic pyramid of Giza, where one could luxuriate in the Edwardian opulence of the rooms. 'Ragged, bedraggled and bearded, our appearance attracted astonished and disapproving glances in the foyer,' recounted Hastings. Once they had secured a room, the pair sped upstairs excitedly planning the evening's entertainment. 'We sped on, found our room, ordered champagne, dinner and the barber …'

Within moments the pair were fast asleep and 'the project so lovingly devised and long awaited faded into oblivion'.

To reach Cairo, Hastings and Mather's party had to cross the treacherous Qattara Depression. Originally the SAS had relied on LRDG guides when operating in this dangerous area.

ANALYSIS

Despite berating his men in the immediate aftermath of the raid on Sidi Haneish, Stirling considered the attack a stunning success. 'Privately I was very pleased,' he told his biographer, Alan Hoe, 'but I didn't want the men to become too blasé about the business. What we had proved to my satisfaction, and it was something I could use to positive effect at MEHQ, was that we could operate under a variety of tactics to the same end.'

Yet the raid on Sidi Haneish proved to be the high-water mark of the SAS in North Africa. When Stirling reached Cairo at the start of August it was to discover that Claude Auchinleck had been sacked by Churchill and replaced by Gen Harold Alexander. There was also a new commander of the Eighth Army, Gen Bernard Montgomery, who was busy planning an autumn offensive against Rommel at El Alamein. Stirling was summoned to MEHQ and informed of what would be expected of the SAS in the forthcoming attack. With the Afrika Korps receiving regular supplies through the ports of Tobruk and Benghazi, Montgomery instructed L Detachment, together with elements of the Middle East Commando and the Special Boat Section (SBS), to raid the port of Benghazi on the night of September 13/14, while a combined force of commandos and infantry would launch a simultaneous seaborne strike against Tobruk.

Stirling was horrified at the plan, considering it anathema to L Detachment's modus operandi. They were suited to small-scale raids, lightning guerrilla warfare, yet the Benghazi raid – codenamed Operation *Bigamy* – was large and cumbersome, consisting of 200 men and a couple of Honey tanks.

Stirling's fears proved well founded. On the approach to Benghazi the force was ambushed and the survivors were forced to race across open desert in the hour before dawn to avoid the appearance of inevitable enemy aircraft. Not all of them reached the safety of the Jebel Mountains 25 miles away. Twelve vehicles were destroyed with the loss of several experienced SAS soldiers, including Capt Chris Bailey, one of the officers on the Sidi Haneish raid, and Cpl David Lambie, one of Mather's faithful gunners, who was captured in the

aftermath of the raid and later drowned when the ship on which he was being taken in chains to Italy was torpedoed by a British submarine.

Stirling was angry with himself for not standing up to MEHQ over what he knew to be a misuse of his force, commenting later: 'It was a sharp lesson which confirmed my previous views on the error of attacking strategical targets on a tactical scale' (Stirling memo, SAS Regt Association). Finally, thanks to the fiasco of Benghazi, MEHQ began to understand how the SAS could best serve its interests in the forthcoming El Alamein offensive. Promoted to Lieutenant-Colonel, Stirling was authorised to expand his unit to regimental status, 1 Special Air Service, comprising 29 officers and 572 other ranks in four squadrons: A under the command of Mayne; B under Stirling; C, a French squadron; and D, an SBS squadron.

Malcolm Pleydell recalled that when he first saw Stirling again after the ill-fated Benghazi raid he was more chipper than he'd expected him to be.

His view was that, since the enemy had known of our raid, none of us could be blamed for what had taken place. But now, he continued, looking round at us eagerly, there was an easy target we ought to be getting busy on: the railway line from Tobruk to Alamein. That should make a lovely objective ... in addition David had some fresh ideas concerning the future of the Special Air Service. He wanted it divided into two squadrons which, by relieving one another, could constantly maintain a force in the rear of the enemy.

Geoff Caton (left) and James McDiarmid on patrol in 1942. Caton was killed in the invasion of Sicily in July 1943.

David Stirling poses with a patrol from B Squadron, just a few weeks before his capture in January 1943.

In October 1942 Paddy Mayne, promoted to Major, led A Squadron into the desert where it operated out of a remote base in the Grand Sand Sea. For three weeks they harassed Axis forces between Tobruk and Matruh, cutting railway lines and attacking vehicle convoys prior to the commencement of the Eighth Army offensive at El Alamein. Once Montgomery launched his great assault against Rommel, A Squadron established a new base at Bir Zelten, further west, where it was joined by Stirling's B Squadron at the end of the month. In the preceding two months Stirling had not only recruited and trained his new squadron, but he had raised another regiment, 2SAS, under the command of his brother, Bill.

A and B Squadron enjoyed a wild party deep in the desert before going their separate ways, with Mayne and A Squadron shooting up retreating enemy transport between Sirte and Agheila, and B Squadron motoring west to attack targets close to the Libyan capital of Tripoli.

Stirling's SAS was now self-sufficient and operating as it chose. Yes, MEHQ had a soft hand on the tiller, but to all intents and purposes the SAS were pirates roaming the desert in search of prey with Mayne and Stirling in charge of their own destinies.

Their wild, intoxicating freedom didn't last long. In January 1943 Stirling was captured as he made an audacious bid to link up with the First Army in

Tunisia, and in the same month A Squadron was withdrawn from the front line, their piracy no longer serving a purpose in a war that was all but won by the Allies.

In the opinion of David Lloyd-Owen, the LRDG officer who had rescued Stirling from the desert in the disastrous aftermath of the inaugural raid, and then suggested a partnership with his own unit, the SAS suffered as a result of its commander's hubris. In his memoirs, *Providence Their Guide*, Lloyd-Owen wrote:

> It is my opinion that from the moment [Stirling] began to get his own transport, and become independent of the LRDG, he began to lose his effectiveness, because he necessarily had to concern himself with the mechanics of administration. David Stirling was a magnificent fighting leader, but the tedious business of worrying where the food, the ammunition, the communications, the fuel and water were to come from was something with which he did not want to concern himself. Up till then the LRDG had done all that for him.

Lloyd-Owen was right. Daring was Stirling's forte, not desk work.

EPILOGUE

Those who took part in the raid on Sidi Haneish never forgot the unique excitement and adventure of the operation, surely one of the most daring of the war in North Africa. Though the raid was insignificant materially in influencing the course of the campaign, it nonetheless inconvenienced the Germans and Italians, causing them to divert men from the front line to help hunt for the raiders and to strengthen airfield defences. When Stirling fell into German hands in January 1943, Rommel wrote to his wife that with his capture 'the British lost the very able and adaptable commander of the desert group which had caused us more damage than any other British unit of equal size'.

So what was the subsequent fate of the men responsible for the first mass jeep attack of the World War II?

David Stirling: Imprisoned in the notorious Colditz Castle, Stirling was released in April 1945 and began planning the SAS's deployment to the Far East. Two atomic bombs curtailed that operation and in October of that year the SAS was disbanded. Stirling emigrated to Rhodesia in 1946 and two years later formed the Capricorn Society, hoping to promote racial harmony in the colony. The end of colonisation interfered with his grand scheme and he returned to the UK in the 1960s, becoming in involved in the security industry. Knighted in 1990, Stirling died a few months later, aged 74.

Paddy Mayne: Unable to resume his rugby career postwar because of a troublesome back, Mayne was a lost soul in Ulster. Though he became president of the Northern Ireland Law Society, his reputation was tarnished by several drink-fuelled incidents north and south of the border. A few days before Christmas 1955 Mayne, aged 40, died in a car crash as he sped through the streets of his native Newtownards on his way back from a bar.

Carol Mather: Captured by the Italians in December 1942, Mather spent nine months as a POW before escaping in the wake of Italy's surrender. He later served on Montgomery's staff during the invasion of France and was awarded an MC during Operation *Market Garden*. Leaving the army

JANUARY 1943

Stirling is captured by the Germans

in 1962, Mather became the Tory MP for Esher in 1970 and stood down in 1987. He was knighted later that year and died in 2006.

Stephen Hastings: Invalided out of the SAS in late 1942 with bronchitis, Hastings joined SOE the following year and worked undercover in both France and Italy. He left the army in 1948 and was recruited by MI6, for whom he worked for a number of years. Elected Tory MP for Mid-Bedfordshire in 1960, Hastings served 23 years in Parliament and died in 2005.

Johnny Cooper: Commissioned in 1944, Cooper spent three months in Occupied France in the summer of 1944 helping wage a guerrilla war against the Germans. He became a career soldier and was awarded an MBE for service in the jungles of Malaya. He finally retired from soldiering in 1966 and died in 2002, aged 80.

Bob Lilley: Fought with the SAS in Sicily, Italy, France and Germany, and a decade later re-enlisted when the SAS was reformed for the Malayan Emergency. Upon leaving the army, Lilley ran a pub in Folkestone and died in 1981.

Malcolm Pleydell: Dr Pleydell left the SAS at the end of the desert war and worked for several months in a hospital in Malta before ill health compelled him to return to the UK. He spent the rest of his working life in the National Health Service and died in 2001.

Gen Bernard Montgomery, commander of the Eighth Army, addresses the SAS in 1943 from the steps of a troopship prior to the invasion of Sicily.

David Lloyd-Owen: Assumed command of the LRDG at the end of 1943 and later fought in the Balkans where he injured his back during a parachute operation. Though the LRDG was disbanded at the end of the war, Lloyd-Owen became a career soldier, retiring with the rank of Major-General. He died in 2001.

Nick Wilder: Wounded during a raid on Barce in September 1942, Wilder finished the war a Lieutenant-Colonel with a DSO. He later returned to his native Waipukurau in New Zealand to farm 1,600 acres. He died in 1970, aged 56

David Russell: He didn't remain long in the SAS, transferring to SOE. In August 1943 Russell was parachuted into Yugoslavia from where he crossed into Romania to make contact with partisans. He was subsequently killed. According to Mike Sadler, 'he was murdered by some partisans for his gold sovereigns he carried.'

Jimmy Storie: Captured in October 1942, Storie spent the rest of the war as a prisoner in the dreaded Stalag VIIIB Lamsdorf and survived a 500-mile Death March in the spring of 1945. He returned to his native Aberdeen on his release and became a tiler. He died in 2012, the last survivor from the inaugural SAS raid of November 1941.

Sandy Scratchley: Upon the reorganisation of the SAS following Stirling's capture, Scratchley's vast experience was transferred to the incipient 2SAS, for which he led several operations into Italy in 1943. After the war he became a highly regarded breeder of racehorses. He died in 1973.

Mike Sadler: Promoted to 1SAS Intelligence Officer in 1944, Sadler was awarded the Military Cross for operations in France. In 1946 he and Paddy Mayne were among the members of an expedition to Antarctica. After a hiatus sailing the world, Sadler spent the rest of his working life with the Diplomatic Service. As of early 2014 he is the sole survivor of the raid on Sidi Haneish. Alas, the camera that he used to take photographs of the raid didn't survive the operation.

BIBLIOGRAPHY

Cooper, Johnny, *One of the Originals* (Pan Books, 1991)

Cowles, Virginia, *The Phantom Major* (Collins, 1958)

Hoe, Alan, *David Stirling* (Warner Books 1992)

James, Malcolm, *Born of the Desert* (Greenhill Books, 1991)

Lewin, Ronald, *The Life & Death of the Afrika Korps* (Pen & Sword, 2003)

Lloyd-Owen, David, *The Desert my Dwelling Place* (Cassell, 1957)

Mortimer, Gavin, *Stirling's Men: The Inside History of the SAS in World War II* (Weidenfeld, 2004)

Moorehead, Alan, *Desert War: The North African Campaign* (Hamish Hamilton, 1965)

Mortimer, Gavin, *The SAS in World War II* (Osprey, 2012)

Mortimer, Gavin, *The Daring Dozen* (Osprey, 2011)

Public Record Office, *Special Forces in the Desert War 1940–1943* (PRO Publications, 2001)

Ross, Hamish, *Paddy Mayne* (Sutton Publishing, 2004)

INDEX